CODE OF
CONDUCT

CODE OF CONDUCT

EVERETT ALVAREZ, JR.
with Samuel A. Schreiner, Jr.

DONALD I. FINE, INC.
NEW YORK

Passages in Chapter XI excerpted from *My Father, My Son* by
Admiral Elmo Zumwalt, Jr., © 1987 by Macmillan Publishing Co.

Library of Congress Cataloging-in-Publication Data

Alvarez, Everett, 1937–
    Code of conduct : an inspirational story of self-healing
  by the famed ex-POW and war hero / Everett Alvarez, Jr., with
  Samuel A. Schreiner, Jr.
        p.   cm.
    Includes bibliographical references and index.
    ISBN 1-55611-310-2
    1. Alvarez, Everett, 1937–.   2. Maryland—Biography.
I. Schreiner, Samuel Agnew.   II. Title.
  CT275.A64A3 1991
  975.2'043'092—dc20
  [B]   91-55183
                                                CIP

Manufactured in the United States of America

10 9 8 7 6 5 4 3 2 1

Designed by Irving Perkins Associates

To my wife, Tammy.

Without her never-ending love,
support and encouragement,
I would not be where
I am today.

Contents

Code of Conduct

For Members of the Armed Forces of the United States

1. I am an American, fighting in the forces which guard my country and our way of life. I am prepared to give my life in their defense.

2. I will never surrender of my own free will. If in command, I will never surrender the members of my command while they still have the means to resist.

3. If I am captured, I will continue to resist by all means available. I will make every effort to escape and aid others to escape. I will accept neither parole nor special favors from the enemy.

4. If I become a prisoner of war, I will keep faith with my fellow prisoners. I will give no information or take part in any action which might be harmful to my comrades. If I am senior, I will take command. If not, I will obey the lawful orders of those appointed over me and will back them up in every way.

5. When questioned, should I become a prisoner of war, I am required to give name, rank, service number, and date of birth. I will evade answering questions to the utmost of my ability. I will make no oral or written statements disloyal to my country and its allies or harmful to their cause.

6. I will never forget that I am an American, fighting for freedom, responsible for my actions, and dedicated to the principles which made my country free. I will trust in my God and in the United States of America.

Executive Order 12633, March 28, 1988
[Signed] Ronald Reagan, President

Prologue

I stood up to the microphones, spread out the sheet of paper with my speech on the lectern and took an appraising glance at the scene before me. It was a gray and blustery day, unusually cold for November in Washington, D.C. Yet here in the open reaches of the memorial mall was a gathering of people standing shoulder to shoulder in an ever widening semicircle that extended beyond the sound of my amplified voice—at least 150,000, according to the crowd counters. I wondered if the words that I had labored over would be adequate to the occasion, if any words could express what we all felt at that moment. We were meeting on that ground to dedicate the Vietnam Veterans Memorial. We—Vietnam veterans and our families and well-wishers—were there to welcome ourselves back to America at last.

The challenge I faced was saying something appropriate to an event that was considered too controversial for the President of the United States to participate in. Although it was November 13, 1982, nearly a decade had not been sufficient time to heal the wounds that the war had inflicted on the home front. The most divisive conflict since the Civil War, the Vietnam War was also its longest, and it had ended in seeming defeat. The black marble wall bearing the names of 58,000 dead was not a gift from a grateful nation. It had been conceived, designed and paid for by the veterans themselves under the inspired leadership of Jan C. Scruggs. This was what the New York *Times* described as "a coming out party given by veterans for veterans."

For me to be standing there as one of the keynote speakers represented the highest honor of my life. I was not appearing in my official capacity as Deputy Director of the Veterans Administration but as an invited guest of the memorial committee, as one of the party givers. A Navy fighter pilot, I had been shot down on the very first raid on North Vietnam and had endured as a prisoner of war in Hanoi for eight and a half years, almost the entire length of the war. The experience had not shaken my faith in my country's cause, and it had deepened my admiration for my fellow fighting men and women. When I returned to America to find the bleeding wounds of divisiveness in my country, and in my own family, I decided to make myself part of the healing process, wherever and whenever possible.

The war wasn't the only issue disturbing and disrupting the America that I rediscovered in the seventies. In the wake of the civil rights struggle, racial, ethnic and economic differences between people were being politicized. As an American of Mexican heritage who had begun life in what today would be called underprivileged circumstances, I was dismayed by this self-limiting polarization. I had tried in my own person and career to represent another kind of America, an America of unity and open opportunity. It was incredible to me that I had survived my prison ordeal, that I had risen to a position where I was regularly sitting in on White House cabinet and budget meetings as part of my daily business, that I was now standing before all of these people as a designated symbol of the two million of us who had served in Vietnam. But all this had happened—was still happening—and nobody knew better than I that I was not special. If I could do it, so could others with a decent code of conduct as a guide.

All these thoughts were tumbling around in my mind as I tried to anchor my paper against the gusts of chilling wind sweeping the mall. I did have a feeling that on this day we might be seeing the beginning of the end of indifference. This ceremony and the parade down Constitution Avenue preceding it climaxed five days of recognition for the sacrifice of Vietnam veterans. A moving part of the recognition had been a reading of the names of the dead in the Washington Cathedral, a service at which President Ronald Reagan did make an appearance. Throughout the week, veterans and the families of the dead met at the wall and allowed themselves to weep, curse, cheer in a long overdue catharsis. Now it was my turn to say what the wall meant to me. I leaned into the microphones.

"The years that have passed since this country ended its involvement in Southeast Asia have been marked by tremendous variations in the mood of the nation. Many Americans today still have a difficult time dealing with that war, its effect on our society and the legacy of those of us sent to fight it. But no one can debate the service and sacrifice of those who fell while serving.

"It is unfortunate that the circumstance under which the more than two million veterans returned from Vietnam did not lend itself to the type of welcome given to veterans of other wars or even to those of us who were prisoners in Vietnam. But with this long overdue week of activities, with this parade today and especially with this dedication, America is saying, 'Welcome home!'

"Here in this great city, the nation's affairs are conducted in buildings new and old that give us both a sense of our history and our destiny. Washington is also a city of monuments, landmarks of stone and statues that testify to the deeds and acts of those who have shaped the nation we have become.

"But the Vietnam Veterans Memorial is unique, vastly different from the monuments to independence and emancipation that flank it. It will be a memorial visible for all time to come to those of us who make and implement our nation's laws and to those who come to this city to see the symbols of our national strength.

"And no one can doubt that the Vietnam Veterans Memorial will be an eternal touchstone for the conscience of this

To Everett Alvarez
With best wishes
pride a respect   *Ay Bush*

When I left the Reagan administration in 1986, then Vice President George Bush and I had a chat that led to my participation in his 1988 campaign. (*Official White House Photograph*)

To Ev Alvarez
With best wishes,

Ronald Reagan

At a White House ceremony in 1988, outgoing President Reagan presented me with the POW Medal while Mrs. Reagan and fellow POW, Senator John McCain, Republican from Arizona, looked on. (*Official White House Photograph*)

nation. It will tell us, as no words can, of the awesome responsibility we have as members of a free and democratic society.

"This memorial is a tribute to all who served in Southeast Asia. It vividly enshrines the memory of those who did not return. And it symbolizes the heroic, unselfish acceptance of duty by millions of Americans who went there.

"The words we speak today are in vivid contrast to the eternal silence of this memorial. That silence, inspired by reverence and respect for those who died and those who served, is in and of itself a tribute.

"There was a time—long ago—when words would have mattered more. But at this place, for all time—it is our hearts that speak.

"I am proud to have served and I am proud to be with you today, and proud to say, 'Welcome home!' "

Since I gave that speech another decade has passed, and the significance of that event on that day has become self-evident. It can be seen in the determination of Americans of all political views to see that those who served in the Gulf War would be accorded a welcome worthy of their courage, a welcome that is unfolding in countrywide celebrations and parades even as these words are being written. Unfortunately, political wars—wars about which honest people honestly differ in opinion, wars thrust upon America by its very nature as a great power—have been, and are likely to continue to be, a hard fact of our national lives. The strength of our country may well be determined by the way we treat those who have elected to serve our country. The desire of young men and women to serve the country will depend upon having the kind of nation undivided in which they can take pride and for which they will be willing to lay down their lives.

I know that it was my own prideful belief in the United States and in the code of conduct to which it subscribes that enabled me to survive with a sense of honor throughout the isolation and torture of long imprisonment. A few years ago I told about that experience in detail in a book entitled *Chained Eagle*. But I have come to realize that the lessons that I and my fellow captives learned about surviving with honor apply to all aspects of personal and national life. What we were before the ordeal, what we have become since, what we still believe, are essential ingredients in understanding the ability to get through life's toughest tests.

Today I travel the country speaking to students, businessmen, political groups, church members, who seem to find that my experiences are relevant to their own. The same techniques and beliefs that served me well in deadly circumstances are applicable to the normal stresses of physical pain, emotional deprivation and despair that can come with illness, job loss, divorce, death of a loved one, disillusionment with leadership or events. As it has happened, they have also proved helpful in dealing with the kind of sudden success and notoriety that is possible in our mercurial society.

In the humble hope that it will continue the healing process begun on that historic day in Washington and that others can learn from my mistakes and successes, I offer this very personal story. The honor that was given me as a spokesman for the millions of brave men and women who served in a war that America should never be allowed to forget is not one that I take lightly. If this book can in any way keep their message alive, it will have served its purpose.

CHAPTER I

Resurrection

IT WAS FEBRUARY 12, 1973. No date could have been more fitting. Although it was coincidental to the event of which I was a part, the date was the 164th anniversary of the birth of Abraham Lincoln, the Great Emancipator. For me it was not only a day of emancipation but of resurrection. After eight and a half years of living death in North Vietnamese prison camps, I was suddenly being set free to resume real life. It should have been a wildly joyous day, but it wasn't. In spite of some loss of weight and prematurely graying hair I still looked like the young Navy pilot who had been shot down on August 5, 1964, during the first sortie of what would become the Vietnam War. Outwardly, I hadn't changed. Inwardly, I was a very different person. Emotionally drained, I could no longer feel joy—or sorrow, either—as I once might have.

Nothing had happened to my mind, I could assess the importance of the day intellectually. When the liberating plane, a giant U.S. Air Force C-141, lifted off the runway of Gia Lam airport at Hanoi and headed southeast over the Gulf of Tonkin toward the Philippines, I could join the rest of the POWs in a cheer. But we soon became silent except for answering the questions put to us by Dr. Roger Shields, the U.S.

State Department representative aboard. Bob Shumaker, who had been imprisoned almost as long as I had, was sitting beside me, and even we had little to say to each other. Each of us was busy with his own thoughts of what lay ahead, and for the most part they were sobering thoughts.

Eight and a half years is a long stretch of time. Think of it as twice the time you spend in college, twice the time between Pearl Harbor and V-J Day, longer than the Reagan presidency. A lot can happen in that much time—and it had. In their effort to turn us into mouthpieces for their propaganda, our captors had fed us only bad news from America. We were shown movies of race riots and peace marches, informed of the assassinations of Robert Kennedy and Martin Luther King, Jr. Only by accident did we learn that this seemingly riven nation had landed a man on the moon. In my case, although they had withheld letters and packages from the family over the years, my jailors had gleefully and immediately passed along the letter from my mother that informed me that my wife had left me, as well as the accounts of my sister Delia's prominent role in the peace movement. Fliers shot down in the last weeks before we were freed, some of whom had still been in high school when I was captured, tried to assure us that things weren't as bad as they seemed. Yet they had to be honest in telling us that veterans returning from Vietnam were getting the cold shoulder—or worse. They thought that it might be different for us, being POWs. "You guys are big names back in the States," they said. But none of us was sure of anything.

Uncertain about so much, and—perhaps fortunately—unfeeling as well, I gave myself over to fantasies about the physical aspects of freedom during that four-hour flight to Clark Air Force Base. Once they realized that we were bargaining chips in the negotiations at Paris that led to our release, the Vietnamese had drastically changed their way of treating us. They gave us more food, allowed us to exercise and fraternize. As a result I was in reasonably good shape. At 143, I was only twenty pounds shy of my preprison weight, and I had good muscle tone from calisthenics and participation in the camp sports that they had allowed the last year of our imprisonment. I was ready for the fruits of freedom. I had thought long and hard about food for years, had literally salivated over a vision of a steak and eggs dinner with all the trimmings. I thought about the bliss of being able to take a hot shower with sweet smelling soap, about sleeping in a soft bed for as long as I liked, about holding a woman in my arms again. Whatever else happened, I could at least look forward to being truly alive in the flesh, and the rest would have to take care of itself.

As the longest held prisoner of war in North Vietnam, I was first on the plane after the sick and wounded had been carried aboard. The thought was that I would also be the first off in the Philippines. I would have to say something that the world was waiting to hear, according to Dr. Shields, who worked his way through the plane to warn us that there would be microphones and cameras, probably a band and certainly a group of dignitaries from the base to meet us. The idea of speaking drove fantasy out of my mind. I was always a shy person, an electrical engineer by education. Performing anywhere but on the athletic field had always been a nervous-making trial for me. I had had some practice in speaking as part of my formal training but not enough for this. *Why did this have to happen today of all days?* I thought. And yet I was torn. Seeing me as spokesman would be a thrill for my parents and sisters watching TV back home in California, some small compensation for all of the anxiety they had been through. It would be an honor for me, too. I had to be honest in admitting to myself that one of my very few sources of satisfaction in captivity had been the recognition I was given by my fellow POWs. When new prisoners were marched through the compound, my cellmates would boost me on their shoulders so that I could be seen over the dividing wall. The message was: look at Alvarez; if he could take it this long, so can you. Well, I would do my best as required by the code of conduct that had sustained me so far.

Just as I was beginning to work up some enthusiasm for my starring role, Jerry Denton—Commander Jeremiah A. Denton, Jr.—got up in front. "There's been a change in plans," he said. "As the senior officer aboard, I'll go off first and say a few words. Then everybody will go off in order of shootdown, Alvie first." Both by rank and age, Denton, a 1946 graduate of the Naval Academy, was senior to a lieutenant junior grade, a 1960 graduate of Santa Clara University, and Denton had been shot down just a year after me. I was disappointed. It was the first of many little alarm bells that would awaken me to the realities of life outside the walls of the Hanoi Hilton, as we sarcastically referred to our last accommodation in enemy land.

The reception at Clark surpassed all the forewarnings about size and volume. There was a band, instruments glittering in the afternoon sunlight. There was a cluster of microphones and cameras. There was a red carpet lined with brass-bedecked officers—and, beyond, a circle of American faces and figures, many of them women and children, yelling and waving flags and holding signs that read WE LOVE YOU. Where were all the people with the cold shoulders? True, it was a military base, but could things be changing again? No longer called on to speak, I did a version of my best by running down the steps and saluting one of the officers whose stripes and bars proclaimed him an admiral. "Lt. (jg.) Everett Alvarez, Jr., reporting back, sir," I said.

A day that had started within the dank walls of the Hanoi Hilton, reeking with human excrement, ended in gleaming white antiseptic rooms of a base hospital where we were taken for preliminary physical and psychological evaluation. For me it was a time of mindless indulgence in sensual pleasures—the feel of the purifying hot shower I had craved, the taste and satiety of a first meal that turned out to be steak, after all, the soft curves and soft voices of the nurses who took care of us, the warm glow from the drinks at a party of celebration. It took me two days to get around to phoning home. I knew that my family could tell from the TV coverage that I was alive and reasonably well. From my point of view, looking out through that Plexiglas emotional shield I had fashioned in self-protection, there was no urgency about establishing closer contact and, in fact, good reason to put it off.

There was no eager wife waiting for my call as I had prayed

for years that there would be. And there was the matter of my sister. Delia and I had been very close right up until the day I left for duty in the Pacific. If what was said about her was true, we would have strong differences in our thinking. We POWs were nearly unanimous in wanting more, rather than less, war in Vietnam. It seemed crystal clear to us that only heavy bombing of the North, especially Hanoi, would bring about the kind of negotiations that finally got us out of there. Even though we could have been killed ourselves, we would cheer in our cells whenever the planes came roaring overhead with their lethal loads. When the camp radio quoted Delia as saying that she had taken action to stop the war because "the war is wrong and is hurting America more than anything else," some of the other POWs gave me a hard time. I defended her for what I was sure was her motive—to get it over with and get us back—and for her right to say what she thought. Wasn't freedom to disagree with the government the thing that made America different from North Vietnam, the thing we were fighting for? Fortunately I had some help in these arguments from Lt. Col. Robinson Risner, our senior ranking officer and a flying ace in the Korean War, since one of his sons was also involved in protesting the war. It was a small comfort to know that I would not be alone in facing a divided family. More of a comfort at the time was that I didn't know how divided they were.

The Navy had suggested to all of the POW families that they have a letter waiting for us in the Philippines to bring us up to date on family matters before we met in person. My mother's letter was carefully written. It did contain some unwelcome—but not surprising—news, such as my grandmother's death several years before. It also contained hints of family problems beyond those I knew about, problems that had been deliberately kept out of the brief letters they were allowed to send me in captivity. My mother thought that it would be better to go into these matters as well as the details of my wife Tangee's defection in face-to-face conversation. I couldn't have agreed with her more. Having just been through the best possible schooling in patience, I had learned to deal with whatever came along a day at a time. So when I finally did get through to my family on the phone I asked no awkward questions and stuck to safe subjects. Typical was an exchange between Mother and me. "Don't be surprised, Mom, I'm getting gray," I told her. "Well, at least, you're not bald," she said. People call me an optimist. With a mother like that, is it any wonder?

After the few days needed for preliminary physical examinations and debriefing—just long enough for them to supply us with new uniforms to grace our arrival in California—we took off from Clark in another C-141 Starlifter. In the middle of the night the plane dropped out of the sky for refueling at Hickam Air Force Base in Hawaii. In spite of the hour the welcome was nearly a repeat of the one in the Philippines. My suspicion grew that the bad news about America had been exaggerated. But for me the Hawaii stop brought an even better surprise—the first contact with good friends from the past. John Nicholson, by then a Captain and Air Operations Officer on the staff of the Commander in Chief, Pacific Fleet, had pulled strings to arrange for a private meeting with him and his wife Evelyn even though it was against regulations because I hadn't been fully debriefed. Maybe it was just as well that we had no audience—the public was spared the sight of two grown men in uniform embracing, and crying.

I couldn't know it then, but those would be the last tears I would shed for years. The shock and surprise of unexpectedly encountering Nick, of all people, on my first landing on U.S. soil penetrated that emotional shield I mentioned earlier. His voice crackling through the radio of my stricken Skyhawk had been the last thing I heard before the explosion of ejection. As operations officer of our Attack Squadron 144 from the U.S.S. *Constellation*, Nick was a section leader on that bombing run at the port of Hon Gai on that, for me, fateful August day. When I had called, "I'm on fire and out of control," Nick had responded, "You know what to do, Alvie." And, keying my mike, I had said, "Right. I'm getting out, I'll see you guys later." Here in Hawaii it was that "later"— approximately 103 months, or 446 weeks, or 3135 days later.

Nick had been more than a companion in combat; he had been a fun-loving selfless friend during carefree days before the war. Once when we were serving together at Lemoore Naval Air Station in California's central San Juaquin Valley, I borrowed Nick's little red MG to go up to San Jose to see Tangee. In an uneven contest with a truck I nearly totaled the car. Lucky as I was to survive the crash with hardly a scratch, I suffered agonies of remorse when I had to call Nick with the bad news. "Forget about the car. How are *you?*" he said at once. He was that kind of friend. Whatever I had been going through since our parting, Nick had had to deal with his own there-but-for-the-grace-of-God-go-I feelings, a kind of survivors' guilt that a lot of military people have to live with at one time or another. It would be hard to say which of us had the greater emotional release at our meeting.

We quickly recovered and camouflaged our feelings with rough banter, he accusing me of keeping my flight leader waiting too long for a debriefing, I accusing him of going off and leaving me with a question that had haunted me all these years: "What did you mean when you said I would know what to do?" I asked.

"I'm not sure, but you did OK," he said.

There was no time then for me to go into detail about my longer ordeal, even if I had felt up to it. I did, though, fill Nick in on what had happened immediately after that radio conversation. No matter how much training you get on the right way to do things, there's no way you can be fully prepared for being blown out of the sky. The manual for ejection, for instance, is written with the thought that your plane will be upright. My crippled plane wouldn't behave, and I had no choice but to blast off halfway upside down. Fortunately, the parachute popped as designed and, even more fortunately, I dropped onto water instead of hard ground. Everything happened in seconds. If my reactions were based on knowledge, it was knowledge turned into instinct. There was one thing, as I told Nick, that I did deliberately. As a boatload of armed Vietnamese approached, firing at me, I tore off my wedding ring and let it sink into the sea. At some point, I had been briefed on the fact that knowledge of a wife or family could become a tool of torture in the hands of interrogators. What a bitter irony to have this recollection surface in the middle of the night in the middle of my return flight to an empty nest!

If they knew about Tangee, the Nicholsons were tactful enough not to bring her name up. Actually, they didn't have much chance since I deliberately steered the conversation in the direction I wanted it to take, a protective technique I would develop into a fine art with everybody close to me in the weeks and months to come. I pumped Nick and Evelyn for news of just about everybody else we knew well at Lemoore or on the *Constellation*. I was hungry for that kind of orientation in the society I was returning to. Nick was frankly amazed that I brought up names that he had forgotten. What he couldn't realize was that playing memory games had proved to be one of the most effective means of maintaining sanity through endless, empty hours. Our tears were long dried by the time my flight was called, and there was no need for more since none of us doubted that we would be seeing each other again.

During the rest of the flight to Travis Air Force Base outside of San Francisco I used the time to write down a few words to say when we trooped off the plane. As a kind of last act as our SRO, Robbie Risner had designated me spokesman, and this time I was sure I would have to go through with it. Instead of trying to meet me amid the hoopla and confusion at Travis, my family had decided to wait for me at our immediate destination, Oak Knoll Naval Hospital, where we would have a quiet, private reunion. But I knew that they would be able to watch the landing from there on TV, and I would be speaking as much to them as to the rest of the country. My hope was that what I said would save a lot of explanation and discussion by leaving no doubt in anybody's mind about what I and my fellow survivors felt about our country. I've kept those words that I jotted down, and they are as true of my sentiments today as they were then:

"For years and years we dreamed of this day and we kept the faith. Faith in God, in our president and in our country. It was this faith that maintained our hope that someday our dreams would come true and today they have. We have come home. God bless the president and God bless you, Mr. and Mrs. America. You did not forget us."

Whatever stirrings of stage fright I might have had as the coast of California came into view were dissipated when the captain of our C-141 invited me up to the flight deck to take over the controls. Although the big plane was clumsy and sluggish to the touch compared to my Skyhawk, the sensation of being aloft and in charge evoked strong memories of the incomparable freedom of flight. It was a sensation that I should have found dangerous since it had lured me into becoming a Navy flier in the first place. But I thoroughly enjoyed it. I decided that, given the opportunity, I would get back into the cockpit again no matter what else happened.

At Travis we were wrapped in a welcome as warm as those

"One happy dude" were the words I scribbled under this picture of me when I first arrived on the American mainland after eight and a half years as a prisoner of war in North Vietnam.

in the Philippines and Hawaii. This was no isolated military installation and the crowd was made up of many of the people I had addressed as "Mr. and Mrs. America." By then I wasn't too surprised to see them there, but I had yet to learn that there was a force in this changing and divided nation called the silent majority. With the cameras and microphones and shouting reporters it was clear that we were instant celebrities. It wasn't at all what we had anticipated. While the cheers were comforting, the limelight was disconcerting. We had been long in a shadowy never-never land where we would dwell for indefinite periods in the dark and alone except for visits from rats and other night-crawling vermin. The only time we saw human beings other than fellow prisoners or jailors was when we were put on display, as in the infamous march through Hanoi. To be transported halfway around the world and put on display as heroes within a matter of days was traumatic. Other celebrities like actors or athletes have role models and a chance to learn how to play their own parts bit by bit. We were totally unprepared.

As if the public reception might not be overwhelming enough, the services also gave us VIP treatment. We had our own coterie of attendants—doctors, public relations people, even junior officers as chauffeurs! For the long drive from Travis to Oak Knoll Hospital they provided official cars. It was uncomfortable riding with strangers who seemed to be studying me as if in search of some sort of hidden damage to my psyche. They meant well, I knew, but they made me feel like a freak. My fault, perhaps. I didn't want to talk, and I didn't. Here I was back in California, only a few miles from where I had been born and raised, and I just wanted to drink in the remembered scenery. It was reassuringly familiar, and I thought: *things have changed—but not all that much*. My emotional shield was firmly back in place, and I didn't let whatever was going through the minds of others in the car worry me. No doubt I appeared traumatized or bafflingly nonchalant, but so what? I was home.

When we pulled up in front of the hospital there was a

band, more cameras, more crowds. No speeches this time but my escorts did indicate that we would have to run the gauntlet into the main entrance to satisfy the media. Right beside the door was a knot of people who were obviously of Mexican background. They were holding a few signs in Spanish, waving a flag. I had seen these symbols in one of the American magazines we were allowed to read just before our release from prison. They accompanied a news story about a farm workers' movement being led by Cesar Chavez.

These people were shouting, "Alvarez! Alvarez!" I paused and somebody ran up to take a picture of me staring at their flag. A woman said in Spanish, "We are so glad to see you. We have been waiting for you. We want to know what you are going to do for us." I had no answer, and I ducked into the building. Even though I had worked in the fields as a youngster, and was of Mexican descent, I didn't much like this assumption that I was automatically a champion of their cause. I felt that I *was one of them* in many ways, but not in political and social-action areas. I was a survivor, not a savior.

The incident started another little alarm bell about the realities of this new life, but it was drowned out by others in the next few hours and days. I was taken to a room that usually held four beds in a bay, but there was only one. This would be my private apartment for as long as I wanted to stay. The medical team hovered around wanting to know when I would be ready to meet my family waiting down the hall. I seemed to surprise them by asking, "Why not now?" Their caution about this meeting made me wonder. Only later did I learn that they had been equally cautious with my family, warning them that I would probably be in a psychological condition that would require them to handle me with emotional kid gloves. So the stage was set for an awkward encounter. When my parents and sisters filed into my room, each hugged me in turn but could find little to say. They all had tears in their eyes, even my tough father. My eyes were dry. This was one more situation that I would have to get through emotionally intact—that is, unfeeling.

February 16, 1973; the family is reunited at Oak Knoll Naval Hospital in Oakland; Mom and Dad are on either side of me; Delia (right) and Madeleine (left) behind us. (*Official U.S. Navy Photo*)

We all pulled our chairs into a circle and I tried to break the ice by going into a big-brother act with Delia. "Well, you've gained weight," I said.

"What a thing to say before you've even said hello," she said.

Madeleine provided safer ground. Only twelve when I left, she had grown into a pretty woman of twenty-one and I had no trouble telling her so. The miniskirt that barely covered her nylon-sheathed legs represented a change in fashion that recently downed pilots had told us we would appreciate. "What have you got on your legs?" I asked. Hiking her skirt another inch to demonstrate, she said, "Haven't you ever heard of pantyhose?" Which at least gave us a shared family laugh.

Nobody questioned me about my time as a POW, and I wasn't in the mood to talk about it. Nor did I ask about what they had been through. I did feel an urge to set something straight. Speaking directly to my father, I said that I could have come home earlier if I had given the North Vietnamese propaganda material, except that I couldn't have lived with myself, couldn't have considered myself a man if I'd done that. I knew that dad would understand and he did. His eyes misted and he said, "You've made me proud." The women said nothing, but I got them involved again by asking about Madeleine's engagement and her wedding plans.

One thing hadn't changed. My parents started arguing over some inconsequential matter, a sound of angry voices that I had heard too often growing up in the close quarters of a small house. I flashed a look at Delia and whispered, "I see they're still at it." She nodded, smiled and then laughed aloud. But there was a bitter note in her laughter and a look in her eye that was a forewarning of what I soon would discover: not only had those years worn away my marriage, but my parents had finally separated and were heading for a divorce. They were pretending to be together at that time only for my benefit.

My meetings with the family in the next few days had more substance. They were hesitant to get into the subject of Tangee, but it no longer, I told myself, bothered me. Unquestionably, the news of her desertion was the hardest blow dealt to me in an imprisonment that included periods of physical torture. Before I was shot down we had only been married for seven months, for much of which time I had been away on duty. In essence we were still honeymooners, and it was the kind of honeymoon that became the stuff of sweet dreams and high hopes for most of that bleak time in prison. Her desertion brought a long down period in prison, but there suddenly came a point when I was given an insight into what waiting must have been like for her. She was not only young and attractive, she was also a dependent sort of person who

I got a kiss from Mother, a hug from Father, as our family was reunited at Oak Knoll Naval Hospital near San Francisco on February 16, 1973.

needed a mate to lean on. Six years of denial had simply been more than her nature could stand. And this understanding gave me a freedom I hadn't known since my bachelor days. I could at least wish Tangee well and write home that I hoped the other man loved her as much as I had. By the time I got home I was left mostly with a curiosity about the details—the timing, the man she had chosen, her child by him, the Mexican—some irony there—divorce. Pumping my family for this information made for talk that wouldn't be confrontational. In any case, I needed the information for the Navy lawyers advising and assisting me in untangling my marital affairs by getting a U.S. divorce.

Dealing with my sister Delia's defection from the cause I'd nearly died for and suffered a long time for was more difficult. Neither of us brought it up at the first meeting, and we might have avoided it entirely except for the media. The Navy had scheduled news conferences with me and my family separately. It was done routinely for all of the POWs. Since the family couldn't be present at mine, Delia came in to see me alone before theirs to check on what I had said. It was good she did. To my annoyance, the reporters were more interested in how I felt about Delia's antiwar activities than anything else. I told her that my response was the same as it had been to my fellow POWs back in Hanoi—her right to speak was one of the things I had been fighting for. I thought that I hid my anger at some of the things she had done—for instance, appearing on the Merv Griffin show with Jane Fonda, one of my least favorite people since her trip to Hanoi—but I learned later that my feelings were almost palpable to Delia. She said, "Let's put it this way . . . if I had been the one in prison, what would you have done?" I had no answer to that. Delia didn't let the silence between us grow. She rushed off to her news conference, where she told the press that we hadn't talked about our disagreements. "I have my beliefs, and he has his, and we can be brother and sister and hold different beliefs," she said. "Contrary to predictions, my brother has not turned against me." So the matter lay uneasily between us, as it did with so many people all over America in those days.

Although my sister
Delia and I embraced
warmly at Oak Knoll,
we would not be able to
reconcile our different
views of the Vietnam
War for years.

On the second night of my stay in Oak Knoll, Joe Kapp, my
best friend from childhood, arrived to take me out on the
town, to show me the lifestyle that had developed in San
Francisco in the sixties—the topless bars, far-out comics,
rock and roll. "Boy, anything you want is yours tonight, Ev,"

he said. Since my only problems seemed to be a need for extensive dental work and the not unexpected discovery of some microbes in my system, I felt ready for some fun, and I couldn't have asked for a better companion. If nothing else, I could learn something about being in the public eye from Joe. As an all-American quarterback at the University of California, Joe had played in the Rose Bowl and had gone on to play in the Super Bowl with the Minnesota Vikings.

Before we hit the high spots Joe and I had a quiet dinner when we caught up on each other's lives. Since we were feeling each other out about the war, it was easier to talk about his first. I soon found out that being a star exacted a price. Acting as a pioneer among the players in the National Football League, he was in litigation over free agency. Although Joe eventually lost his own battle in court, the war he helped to start was won for other players. When we got around to me, he asked, "Everett, how was it? You know, this war was damn confusing. Nobody back home knew what was going on. Did they hurt you?"

It was obvious that he was personally confused but I did try to tell him a little about the lousy food, the loneliness in solitary, the beatings. An emotional person, Joe started to scowl and clench his fists. "How could they do that to you? How could you stand it?"

I didn't want him to get upset and ruin the evening, so I tried to explain it to him as I had once done with a new cellmate in Hanoi. I told him it was a little like playing football. You do get hurt but you get through it; you don't feel it too much if you keep your mind on the game. He nodded and then switched subjects with a kind of relief. "Hey, now that you're here, Everett, I hope you'll come down and talk to my kids. I promised them I'd try to bring you."

He then launched into an enthusiastic description of the work he was trying to do with young Hispanics in the towns along the Mexican border, where he was a big hero because he was half-Mexican. He also expressed sympathies for the embattled farm workers. It was a reprise of the scene at the hospital door that I wasn't ready for. Growing up together in Salinas, Joe and I never thought of ourselves as just Mexican or Hispanic. In fact, most of our other friends were the Anglos we had played football and other sports with, the men now on the management side of the farm battle. I realized then that I was as confused about the struggle here as Joe was about the one in Vietnam. I told him that I didn't have any idea about what I would be doing or where I would be after I got out of the hospital but that right then and there what I wanted to do was see the sights.

Joe was a good guide, and it was wonderful to be out among free people whooping it up and having a good time. Along in the wee hours we ended up going from club to club on Union Street. In one of them there were a lot of French sailors on leave from a ship in port. When I heard them talking I said, "Joe, come on over with me and say hi to those guys." I had picked up a pretty good working knowledge of French from our self-taught prison language classes. Joe was impressed when he heard me rattling it off. Scoring one up on Joe, who had always been bigger and better than I in our youthful games, was a final plus for the evening. It also had me wondering as we drove back to the hospital: what else had I, unconsciously, learned in those seemingly lost years that would apply to my new life?

CHAPTER II

Reentry On the Fast Track

To MAKE LIFE ENDURABLE in prison you learn to live either in the past or the future. And this involves an exercise of memory or imagination, and both of these out-of-body capabilities get a good workout over a period of years. Although I was able to astonish others like Nick Nicholson, and sometimes myself, with feats of memory, I have to admit that my imagination fell far short of picturing the bursts of activity that lit up the days and nights while I was supposedly recuperating at Oak Knoll Naval Hospital. In a complete reversal of my time structure, the present was so crammed with new adventures and excitements that I had no time, or inclination, to dwell on the past or think about the future. My "celebrity" status had not ended with a few words spoken in front of the cameras at the airport. Through the accident of circumstances not of my making, I was, I realized, looked on as a hero. There wasn't anything I could do about it. It was a fact to be faced. In some ways I had little more control over what began happening to me in freedom than I had had in prison. The big difference, of course, was that most of these new experiences were pleasant, even exhilarating.

From the first I was conscious of serving as a kind of symbol. Since I was the first pilot to have been shot down over North Vietnam it was easy for people to single me out for honors that were really meant for all of the survivors who came back with me. Knowing this and keeping it in mind helped me put all the attention in perspective, although, frankly, I didn't let it keep me from enjoying most of it. Symbols, of course, are expected to have a certain shine, and I was made conscious of that at one of the first of the honoring ceremonies. It was an "Alvarez Day" in Santa Clara, a community just south of San Francisco where our family home had been established while I was attending Santa Clara University. The day was to begin with the dedication of a park named for me and end with a banquet at the university.

Although Salinas, further to the south, was where I had been born and spent my growing-up years, Santa Clara was where I had gone through an intense time of intellectual awakening. The university, a Jesuit institution with an all-male undergraduate body of about a thousand students when I went there had also provided the means for a spiritual growth that had been a source of strength during my years as a POW. Even the university's physical environment with its old mission chapel and vine-shaded walks had been conducive to religious meditation. I owed a lot to Santa Clara, and it was the right place to begin my reentry into a changed America.

The park was conveniently located just around the corner from my mother's house on Bohannon Drive, so the crowd of about eight hundred that gathered under a gray sky for the event was heavily sprinkled with neighbors as well as members of the press. Master of ceremonies was Santa Clara's young mayor, Gary Gillmor. We hadn't met before even though Gary had also attended Santa Clara University a few years ahead of me. In spite of being in a postarrival daze I managed to get out a few words about how honored I was to have a park named after me where kids could enjoy themselves. Then came what I've since learned to call a "photo op" when Gary and I were maneuvered into position beside the newly minted sign proclaiming the area as EVERETT ALVAREZ, JR., PARK. While the cameras were snapping and grinding away, Gary put his arm around my shoulders and whispered, "Don't mess up, Ev. If you do, we'll have to change that sign." The last I heard, the sign is still there.

The banquet at the university that evening was something of a fateful occasion. I met James Shea, a trustee of Santa Clara University and a vice-president of Southern Pacific Railroad. We had a lot in common. Although I hadn't known him at school, Jim's oldest son, James Patrick, had been a year behind me at Santa Clara, had also become a pilot, had also been shot down in a raid over North Vietnam in 1965. But young Jim had been killed, leaving a widow Susan and a daughter Kelly. Another son had been serving as an enlisted man on the *Constellation* when I took off for my last flight. There was such an instant rapport between Jim Shea and me that he took me on as a surrogate son.

Another older man who virtually adopted me at that banquet was Father Walter Schmidt. Father Schmidt was vice-president of the university and founder of Santa Clara Youth Village. Popular among the stars, he had no trouble enlisting the likes of Frank Sinatra, Andy Williams, Sammy Davis, Jr., for his Golden Circle Theater fund raisers to support the university. Both of these men would have a hand in shaping my life after Nam.

So would Ronald Reagan. Then governor of California with an eye on the White House, Reagan hosted a party for the California POWs. We were asked to bring a wife or mother or date. In view of their well-known stand against the war I didn't think that either my mother or Delia would be comfortable in a crowd of POWs, and there was always a chance of an embarrassing incident if Delia crossed words with one of them. Madeleine was a different story. Too busy getting herself through the troublesome teens to bother her head about politics, she was thrilled to be asked. When she showed up at the hospital dressed to the nines, I knew I'd made a good choice. Nancy Reagan, who had done her homework and was aware of my symbolic status as the longest survivor in North

I took my younger sister Madeleine to a reception for California POWs at Governor Ronald Reagan's home in Sacramento in March, 1973. (*BEE Photo*)

Nancy Reagan's warm greeting at the reception in Sacramento was the beginning of a fateful friendship for me. (*BEE Photo*)

Vietnam, greeted me at the door of the governor's mansion in Sacramento with a hug that turned into another photo op.

During the reception and dinner I met another person who would become significant in my life—Nancy Reynolds, the Reagans' social secretary. An exuberant livewire who had been a TV news anchor in San Francisco, Nancy Reynolds knew how to make a shy person feel at home. At one point she maneuvered me into an informal private session with the governor and Mrs. Reagan. It was a chance to tell them a story from my prison experience that I had been saving for such an opportunity if it ever arose. During interrogations, the North Vietnamese would often rant and rave about war criminals. In fact, they always considered us war criminals instead of prisoners of war, and they would usually wind up by saying that the man in the White House—first Johnson, then Nixon—was the greatest war criminal, the world's Public Enemy Number One. When Reagan became governor he issued a statement in support of the troops in Vietnam, and I was called on the carpet.

"Where is your home? Where do you live?" an interrogator asked me.

"In California."

"Who is governor of California?"

"Ronald Reagan."

"Ah, Reagan! Ah, yes, I know," he said nodding his head. "He is truly World's Public Enemy Number One!"

Apparently a little surprised by my story, Reagan sat up straighter, shoulders back, and said something like, "Oh, well . . ."

I said, "So you see, Governor, you are in a very special class with Nixon and others like us who are war criminals. But you are really the biggest of all criminals, in Vietnamese eyes."

Both Reagans laughed, and the story became part of Reagan's repertoire. From what I've heard, he told it much better than I did. I drifted off again into the crowd, where I met Ed Meese and Mike Deaver. A few days after that party I got a call at the hospital from Nancy Reynolds. "The Reagans really enjoyed meeting you," she said. "Mrs. Reagan is always asking about you, Ev, and wants to know how you're doing. Come on up here and I'll buy you a lunch." At the time I had no appreciation of the force and direction of these seemingly casual contacts.

But everything wasn't all formal and ceremonial. Mail was delivered to my hospital room in bags, and I had to ask family members to winnow through it. There were letters, often with pictures, from young women who wanted to meet me. Occasionally, I actually called the most promising ones. Frankly, once burned, I was only looking for some entertaining female companionship. I hadn't had either the time or money to play the dating game as a teenager and college student, and I enjoyed getting a belated chance at it. A little female attention did a lot for my confidence. As a so-called celebrity I discovered that even my private life could become public. Local gossip columnists would speculate on the identity of the lady seen dancing at such-and-such establishment with Everett Alvarez.

A byproduct of all of this activity was that it prevented me from facing up to family problems. We weren't together often, and I was seldom alone with any of them. Somehow or other the right time and place for an open honest discussion of our different experiences and differences in thinking didn't happen. Instead of bringing us together my coming home seemed to be widening the gap between us. In addition to disagreements about the war, there was the Chicano movement. Delia and several of my cousins were actively involved, and this had naturally led to expectations that I would want to join them. The more publicity I got the more I was pressured to declare my stand in this confusing sociological, political rift that had developed while I was cut off from reality.

When I was growing up I would hear friends or relatives of the family—recent immigrants or first-generation Americans—refer to each other as Chicanos. The word had no political connotation. It was just easier to say "He's a fellow Chicano" instead of "He's a Mexican-American." Another term was *La Rasa*, The Race. This came out of the history of Spanish settlement in Latin America. Instead of bringing wives and families, as the settlers of North America had done, the Spanish brought the church, whose mission was to convert the native population and many of the Spanish married Indians. The children of these marriages considered themselves a new group and called themselves *La Rasa*. To me words like Chicano and La Rasa meant people who had come from Mexico. Period. I didn't like the sound of a "Chicano movement" or a "Chicano manifesto." The Salinas I grew up in without ever thinking about being different was being torn apart, turned into a political hotbed.

One time I returned a call-message left at the hospital, hoping it was from a young lady. Instead it was a man who spoke with a heavy Spanish accent.

"Commander Alvarez," he said, "you're our hero down here in the San Joaquin Valley. Yes, sir, you're our hero. We've got all of these kids who look up to you, and we want you to be the guest of honor at our fiesta. You'll come, won't you?"

"Let me check it out," I said.

Navy public relations officers were helping me screen invitations, and I asked them to check out the man. It turned out that he was a legitimate leader in the migrant workers' union. From firsthand knowledge in my youth, I knew about the tough economic and social conditions of migrant workers, the need for great improvement. But I was also bothered by certain political overtones of the movement. I didn't like its divisiveness, its relentlessly negative attitude. I was mulling over the invitation when I got a call from a newspaper editor in the valley. "I understand you're going to be over here for the fiesta."

"I was invited but I haven't made up my mind," I said.

"Well, there's this fella who's advertising on the radio and letting us know he wants some advertising in the paper that you are going to be here."

Apart from my concern about how the man might use me, his automatic assumption that I would come plain irritated me. "That's the man who called and I only told him I was checking it out. I've decided not to go," I told the editor, but I felt conflicted, if not guilty.

Although I managed to stay firm in that instance, I didn't want to appear insensitive to Hispanic issues. The next invitation was from the Bay Area Latin American Manufacturers Association, a local organization. All they wanted me to do, they said, was to join them for a banquet in a local restaurant and receive an award. Even my sister Delia approved. "If you go let me join you." I was glad that she did. As soon as we showed up in the restaurant a man came running over with a TV crew trailing him. "Uh, oh," Delia said, "he's running for mayor." Delia stepped between us and waved them away.

Out hosts led us to the seats on the dais, where there were programs between the cutlery. Hitting me right in the eye were the words GUEST SPEAKER—COMMANDER ALVAREZ. "What's this?" I asked one of my hosts.

"Oh, that's OK, just say a few words."

Delia shot me a boy-have-we-been-had look. After a dinner I could hardly taste, the chairman stood and said, "And now, ladies and gentlemen, the moment we have been waiting for—Commander Alvarez."

The lights went out, the cameras went on, I got to my feet. I knew none of the people. I knew nothing about their organization or what it stood for. I managed to get out a few words—a very few—about how I was glad to be there and to be home, and I wished them well. After I sat down, the payoff was quick in coming. A business man called from the floor, "Because Commander Alvarez is here I donate $500." Another jumped up and said, "I'll give $1,000." And on and on. I could hardly wait to get out of there and back to my hospital room. I had lost my virginity as a celebrity, and there was no denying it. When I turned on the ten o'clock news, there I was endorsing an agenda I knew nothing about.

Not long after that there came an invitation about which I had no hesitation. On the phone from Los Angeles was John Gavin, who was then president of the Screen Actors Guild. He wanted me to be his guest at the Academy Awards. "I'll get you a date," he said.

"OK," I said. "I'm five ten."

"In that case I'll get you a six-foot-two blonde." I decided I would like this guy.

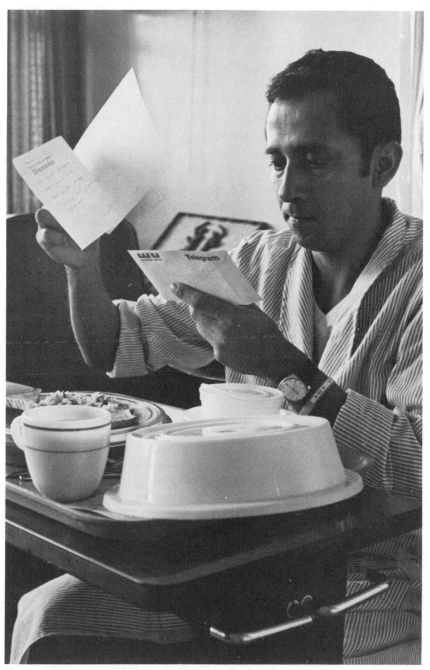

From the moment of my arrival at Oak Knoll Naval Hospital, there came a flood of letters from well-wishers, including a number of young women I later dated.

Movies had been a major source of entertainment in my childhood. In fact, I became a flier mostly because of those old movies glorifying fliers in *Flying Tigers, God Is My Co-pilot, The Bridges at Toko-Ri*. Whether he produced a statu-esque blonde or not, Gavin would, I figured, at least turn up some of my celluloid heroes. And maybe the women who inspired young men's dreams.

From the moment I landed in Los Angeles I felt like I was going through a movie myself. A limousine picked me up at the hotel and took me off to lunch with my host. A suave, handsome man who would later put his charm and negotiat-ing ability to use as the U.S. Ambassador to Mexico, Gavin put me immediately at my ease. My date, he informed me, was a starlet from New York who would be going all-out to make an impression on everybody, including me. Our group would consist of me and my date—call her Susie—Gavin and his girlfriend Connie, who later became his wife, Gavin's assistant and his date Linda. A limousine would collect us and go on to the Dorothy Chandler Pavilion, where the assis-tant would meet us.

All this was taking place on March 27, 1973, the day that the last of the POWs were being released back in Vietnam. It was also a day when Watergate conspirator E. Howard Hunt, Jr., appeared before a federal grand jury in Washington to begin secret testimony, when Indians were shooting it out with FBI agents at a place called Wounded Knee in South Dakota, when U.S. troops were being withdrawn from South Vietnam while American pilots of a new generation were conducting controversial bombing raids in Cambodia. I was aware of all of this front-page news, but that tight-in-place emotional shield kept it from the front of my consciousness.

Susie, my date, was a stunner. When we started mingling with the celebrities, the big surprise of the evening for me was to discover that I was a main attraction. John Wayne greeted me with a warm handshake, Ricardo Montalban with a hug. Some asked for *my* autograph. It was a heady experience for a boy from the wrong side of the tracks and recently sprung from the Hanoi Hilton.

The warm glow I got from these greetings was chilled a bit during the ceremonies when Marlon Brando's surprise was sprung. He was voted best actor, and he had arranged for an Apache Indian girl named Sasheen Little Feather to receive his Oscar as a protest against the way Hollywood had "been responsible for making a mockery of Indians." With the guns still popping at Wounded Knee, it was certainly a dramatic gesture. I had the same uneasy reaction I was having about the Chicano movement. Potentially it was a divisive tactic. And maybe a bit of a grandstand play.

When we went to a party afterward, Susie, the New York "starlet," roamed the room. In the midst of what little conversation we could make, she would suddenly say, "Oh, there's so-and-so," jump up and dart across the room, come back and repeat the performance. She was like a yo-yo. It didn't matter. I was enjoying Linda and Gavin's Connie, women who had things other than themselves on their minds. I would be in for more serious business within hours, and the whole event was a welcome diversion.

The next morning I received a request from the Navy to be on the East Coast for a news conference on the 29th. Until all of the POWs were released or accounted for it had been official policy for all of us to avoid discussing our prison treatment publicly. By revealing the truth about it we might bring reprisals on those still being held. But with the last of our prisoners leaving on the day I was in Los Angeles, the wraps were off. The government didn't want to lose any time letting the public know the nature of the enemy we had been facing. Since there was also going to be a West Coast news conference, it puzzled me that they would fly me across the continent. But unquestioning obedience is part of the military code, and I was grateful to be included among those who would speak for our comrades.

Right after that the phone rang again in my hotel room, and at the other end of the line was Nancy Reynolds. She was in town to arrange a party for the Reagans, who were staying in a house loaned to them by Justin Dart. The Reagans insisted I come to their party, she told me when I told her about my other "party" in Bethesda, Maryland, about twenty-four hours away. "That isn't until tomorrow. You've got all night to get there," Nancy argued. "C'mon, Ev. Get yourself a date and come to the party. I'll get hell from Nancy Reagan if you don't." The Navy public relations people said no sweat, they'd have a car waiting at the Reagans' to take me to the airport in time to catch the Red Eye. But what about a date? Even if she weren't on her way back to New York, Susie was out of the question. The only other woman I knew in Los Angeles was Linda. She had given the impression that she wasn't altogether attached to Gavin's assistant, but how would she react to an early morning-after call with a last-minute invitation? I called her at work. She paused only a few seconds before saying yes.

Much more comfortable than I had been at my first Reagan party, I had a relaxed time, particularly with Mrs. Reagan. I found her very warm in contrast to her public image. Door prizes were given out at the party. Mine was a large coffee-maker, something I could really use. I crammed it into the front seat alongside my Navy officer chauffeur when he came to pick me up. Linda was nice enough to insist on riding to the airport with me, and I had a minor inspiration—a perfect excuse for seeing her again by asking her to take charge of the coffeemaker until I got back. I hope she's been able to make a lot of good coffee with it over the years because I was never to see her or my prize again, thanks to circumstances that have convinced me of the truth of the old saying that life is what happens when you have made other plans.

There were two news conferences in the Washington area. Robbie Risner and some others held forth at Andrews Air Force Base in Maryland, and I was with a group at Bethesda Naval Hospital. For the first time we talked about torture. Risner said that he had been tied into a ball so tight that his toes pushed against his mouth and his shoulders popped out of their sockets, and yet he said truly that a stretch of six months of solitary was harder to take. I remembered what it felt like being forced to sit for days on a stool without sleep or food. All of us admitted to having made or signed statements for propaganda purposes when we were pushed beyond our limits. I confessed reaching a point where I decided that refusing to sign a preposterous statement wasn't worth dying for, and then wishing later that I had died instead of yielding. This guilt would have been intolerable if we each hadn't learned through our camp-communications system that the others were also, at some point, yielding. Our senior officers like Risner, in fact, went along with modifying the code of conduct to permit this. The difference between the rest of us and the few turncoats among us was that we never agreed to do anything *willingly*, enduring some form of torture each time, and we never accepted favors for "good behavior"—the ultimate being early release. An eerie echo of all this came back to me eighteen years later when I saw the first pictures of battered POWs reading propaganda on Baghdad TV during the Gulf War. I knew then that their words had been forced, but they, too, had to wait until all were released to give details. In that same Bethesda hospital I would meet with the Navy and Marine POWs from Iraq, and I can only hope that I was able to help them with their feelings of guilt by telling them about our experiences.

They didn't have luxury shops at the "Hanoi Hilton," our prison in the enemy capital, so I brought home only these sorry souvenirs of my stay. They are now in the Navy museum in Washington.

Before the summons to Bethesda, my plans had included being in Salinas, where I grew up, for a welcome-home affair on the 30th. I had been booked for a return flight out of Baltimore to San Francisco at 10:00 A.M. that day. That would be cutting it fine, so as soon as I arrived in the East I asked the people making arrangements to try for an earlier flight. They managed to get me on a 9:00 A.M. United Airlines flight from Washington's Dulles Airport. The first indication that providence had a hand on the switch came at the counter as I checked in about an hour ahead of time. "Commander Alvarez," the ticket agent said, "you have been upgraded to first-class." Before I could even thank him a young woman appeared at my elbow and introduced herself as Tammy Ilyas, a United passenger service representative.

She invited me to come to her office for coffee while I waited for the flight, explaining as we walked along that making VIPs happy with United's service was her job. She said that orders had come down from the top at United to treat all of us POWs as VIPs, which accounted for my being upgraded. At the time, it also seemed to account for the fact that she knew a good deal about me. She was professionally expert at putting people at ease. Guessing rightly that a pilot would be interested in new airplanes, she told me all about the DC-10s and 747s that had come into service while I was gone. I couldn't believe that an hour had passed when she said that it was time to go. At the gate she handed me her business card with her private phone number. "Call me if you get back to Washington," she said.

Nice girl, I thought as I settled into my first-class seat. I had an even better thought about her when the attendant greeted me by name and popped the cork of a complimentary bottle of champagne. I gratefully tucked Miss Thomasine Ilyas's card away in my wallet for future reference.

CHAPTER III

The High Road to Romance

DURING THE SPRING and summer of 1973 I seemed to be forever in the air, covering California and crisscrossing the country to keep one engagement after another. In between flights I stayed at Oak Knoll until my dental work was completed in mid-May and then moved into my mother's house in Santa Clara. Nothing I did could be considered work in the usual sense since I was officially using up accumulated Navy leave. I was free to set my own agenda, and I tried to make the most of it. I had been a football player and track man, but they had named a golf tournament at Lemoore Naval Air Station for me when I was in captivity and I thought I ought to practice so I wouldn't look too bad in the tournament. I was becoming an activity junkie.

Like my plastic emotional guard, being constantly on the go was a form of psychological protection. As long as I had something lined up for the next hour, the next day, I didn't have to think about the uncertain future or bog down in regrets about the lost past. I continued to avoid meaningful conversations with my mother and sisters and saw very little of my father, who was busy creating his own life outside the family. I made no effort to get in touch with Tangee, leaving

Since I wasn't ill, life was so hectic during those months in the hospital that I had a hard time finding moments of contemplation like this.

After years dressed in nothing but prison pajamas, one of the first things I did was to outfit myself with comfortable civilian clothes.

that to the Navy lawyers and the outside counsel that they engaged to handle our divorce. This legal involvement led indirectly to another experience that would have a profound influence on me.

Before I was released from prison a Los Angeles literary agent named Irving (Swifty) Lazar had approached my sister Delia about my writing a book. I would guess that all of us had given some thought during our prison time to what kind of story we had to tell and how to do it. This thought was best expressed by another Navy flier, Lt. Gerald (Jerry) Coffee. We had a somewhat special relationship based on being from neighboring towns. He was called the Modesto Flash, I the Salinas Streak. He was the first pilot shot down in 1966. One day we were both in a futile argument with two turncoats who had willingly swallowed and were regurgitating Vietnamese propaganda. We tried to convince them that we all owed our survival to sticking together as a group, to hanging onto our faith in God and our country. I was very discouraged that we didn't get anywhere with them, but Jerry took a brighter view. "Boy, Everett," he said, "have we got a message. Have we got a story to tell people back home." The notion that telling our story of surviving by sticking to our values would do some good was a morale booster; it made our days at the Hanoi Hilton seem less useless. With this in mind, I didn't feel that I could turn down a chance to publish a book without at least some investigation.

I wasn't much more of a writer than a speaker. The kind of writing skills that I had learned as an engineer weren't the same I would need for a book, and I knew nothing about book publishing. I mentioned the matter to my attorneys, who introduced me to a lawyer specializing in literary work, Howard Nemerovski. By probing around a little, Howard came up with an offer of $25,000 in advance for a book about my experiences, but he thought that I could do better.

"Go down to LA and see Swifty," he advised. "But be prepared. He'll pick you up at the airport, probably in a limo, and take you to the Beverly Hills Hotel for lunch. What he wants is for people to see that you're with him. After that he'll take you to his home to see his art collection. Let him talk, but let any final decision come up between you and me."

I went to Los Angeles, and the day went as predicted until Howard himself added a surprise touch. Midway through lunch the waiter came to our table with a phone. The call was for *me*. It was Howard: "Has he said anything to you?" I said, "No." Howard said, "Well, let me know," and hung up. Obviously, Howard just wanted Mr. Lazar to know that he was dealing with a person of some importance, a person "in touch." As it turned out, Lazar's proposition was to take me to New York for a week and to introduce me to all the top publishers. I didn't see that I had anything to lose and agreed. Lunch was suddenly over with no mention of the art collection. In the mood for the full treatment, I asked, "May I see your art collection? I hear wonderful things about it." Lazar didn't flinch; he conveyed me by limousine to his hilltop home overlooking the city and let me see his treasures before sending me off to the airport.

In that New York week we were warmly received by the top people in every major publishing house. But a problem that developed immediately was that I didn't know what was expected of me. After introductions Swifty would say, "Everett here has a great story to tell." The publishers would just stare at me, and I would fumble around saying that I had in mind a sort of Stalag 17 thing, an account of how we survived on a day-to-day basis by developing communications codes, helping each other, following our senior officers' directions to make them torture us for propaganda and so on. If they didn't actually yawn, their eyes would glaze over until somebody, usually Swifty, brought up the fact that my wife had run off with another man and my family had been active in antiwar protests. I could see their interest come alive then, and I cringed. I didn't even want to talk about those things, let alone write about them. When they got the message they politely ushered me to the door.

The whole thing climaxed in a particular publisher's office. The occasion was an informal lunch—sandwiches ordered up from a deli. It was all very friendly. The young publisher, dressed in an open shirt and jeans, sat on the floor; Swifty and I shared the sofa. Like all the others, this man's interest centered on my relationship to antiwar activities, and he asked, "Tell me, Ev, how do you feel about Jane Fonda, about the delegations that went to Hanoi?" My feelings about Jane Fonda were definitely not friendly. I hesitated before answering, picturing in my mind the propaganda film that our captors had shown us of her visit to North Vietnam. I clearly remembered the shot of her with a North Vietnamese helmet on, peering through the gunsight of an anti-aircraft weapon, then embracing the Vietnamese gunners. Knowing my feelings, Swifty said, "Be careful, Ev. She's a good person. Be careful what you say."

I was careful all right. I didn't trust myself to say anything. I don't know whether I was more enraged or hurt. The man was my agent, supposedly on my side, but he was defending Jane Fonda. Walking down the street with Lazar after that lunch, I said, "I think maybe I'll go home." He didn't argue with me. After promising an advance of eighty or a hundred thousand dollars, Lazar now said, "You know Howard doesn't have a lot of experience in this field yet. He should have grabbed that $25,000."

When I got on the plane to San Francisco I was disappointed and discouraged—not because there would be no book bonanza but because of this additional evidence of a huge gap in understanding between us POWs and the rest of the country. These publishers wanted to look into a can of worms that I wasn't about to open. Well, a book can wait, I thought. The best books about World War II are still being written. If I have a good story to tell, it will still be there ten or fifteen years from now. I wasn't allowed to be alone with my gloomy thoughts for very long. People on the plane recognized me. One offered me the keys to his house and boat in Biscayne, Florida. As with the airport receptions, I was reminded that there were Americans who saw in us a reason for pride, and I took some fresh pride in myself for not giving in to those publishers.

I was really more interested in getting on with my new life

than doing the kind of brooding over the past that a book would require. Coming up soon was an intriguing and very special event. Riding high in the air on a cross-continent flight was an appropriate place to dwell on the image of Tammy Ilyas, as I remembered her, and the mysterious way our lives seemed to be entwining. For example, a few weeks after I had met Tammy at the United Airlines counter in Dulles Airport I was on the dais at a testimonial dinner that the Jaycees of Carmel Valley were giving me when Congressman Burt Talcott slipped me a note from Tammy reminding me to call her. How did Burt know her? "Oh, everybody in Washington knows Tammy. She's a wonderful girl," he said.

It was a good endorsement from a person I had known for years, and it was *very* nice to know that Miss Ilyas remembered me. But I was in California and she was in Washington. There wasn't much future in that. Next there came a command invitation from the White House. President Nixon was planning a party for all of the POWs in late May. My greatest wish on returning to the United States—a chance to shake Mr. Nixon's hand and thank him for my freedom—was being granted. Afraid that it never would, I had tried to express my feelings in a letter that I doubted would ever reach his eyes:

"It was my belief in all the intrinsic values which are inherent in just being an American, faith in my God, my fellow Americans, and you, Mr. President, that carried me through these long years of imprisonment," I had written. "These thoughts sustained me when considerable pressure was applied by our captors to sway our convictions. I did not waiver. In my mind there was only one mode of conduct, one answer to our captors when questioned, and one way to come home—with our honor and our dignity. The courageous decisions you made in resolving difficult problems undoubtedly helped achieve a proper settlement. For this, Mr. President, I want to thank you. With the greatest respect and heartfelt appreciation, I want to thank you for bringing us home the only way we could—with our pride, our dignity and our honor."

As with Governor Reagan's affair, we were asked to bring

along what would be called these days "a significant other." I thought immediately of Tammy Ilyas. She would no doubt feel right at home in a White House atmosphere, and with her dark hair, trim figure and dazzling smile would make quite an entry. I didn't have much trouble convincing her to go—in fact, she acted as if she had expected my call. Before we got off the phone we agreed that I would come early so that she could show me around Washington while we got better acquainted before the grand affair. With that to look forward to I soon forgot the book fiasco.

My immediate involvement after getting back from New York was learning to deal with life outside Oak Knoll, which had become a cocoon for me. Having Navy personnel to help me and front for me on a daily basis, it was easier to stand on neutral ground in the political turmoil around me. Along with the numerous family members who were active in the Chicano movement, old high-school friends, now owners and managers of the farms and other enterprises under assault, approached me to act as an intermediary. People from both ends of the political spectrum were proposing that I use my exposure to run for office. I took a hands-off position with both sides. I had to. I had decided to turn military service into a career. So politics was out. Although I had signed on for only five years, that deadline had passed while I was in prison. I had come out a lieutenant commander, two ranks up on the scale, more than halfway along toward a twenty-year retirement and with several options about higher education and type of service. Staying in service looked like the way to go.

As for politics, I had undergone a sea change during captivity that further widened that gap between me and my family and many old friends and associates. I had grown up in a community that had been solidly Democratic since the days of the great Depression. I had cast my first vote for Kennedy not only in keeping with this tradition but because I was attracted by his youth and vitality. But from the viewpoint of the Hanoi Hilton, national politics in America took on a very different look for me and for almost all of my prison mates.

Lyndon Johnson's waffling on the war and withdrawal from the race in 1968 did not sit well with us. McGovern's attitudes in 1972 that were passed along to us with glee by our torturers as proof of America's weak will were terrifying. Not one of us believed that the war was being prosecuted as it ought to be. It was like playing football without being able to cross the fifty-yard line. Only as Nixon persisted with his bombing did we begin to have hope and finally gain our freedom. When people would ask me about my politics after I got back, I would say: "I was a Democrat until somebody started shooting at me and then I became a Republican real fast." It wasn't a joke. I had wanted to see Nixon reelected in 1974, and I was willing to take a stand on that.

I didn't, though, think either party had a monopoly on all the right answers. With my background I couldn't help but be aware of great areas of unfairness and injustice in our society, and I looked for a nonpolitical way to put my position to some good use in these areas. In connection with this, living back in Santa Clara in my mother's house was a bit serendipitous. Being near the university, I saw a lot of Father Schmidt, who advised and helped me in setting up a scholarship foundation at Santa Clara for needy students, part of which I would fund with honoraria from speaking engagements. Since education had proved to be the way up and out not only for me and my sisters but a number of my cousins, I couldn't think of a better contribution on my part to the cause of Mexican-Americans or any other disadvantaged people. Getting to know Father Schmidt better would also have an effect on me that I couldn't possibly foresee at the time.

Although I prepared for the Washington week by exchanging letters with Tammy Ilyas, I still didn't burn bridges in California by giving up dating. I might have saved a lot of time and money if I had. Although I had been impressed from the first by Tammy's poise, charm, and more, it would take a while for me to become aware of her power. She is a determined and persistent person who goes after what she wants—and usually gets it. In that we are pretty much alike in spite of differences in style. Tammy was the first to recognize this, but I at least sensed it, because my interest in seeing her again was far from casual.

In the days we spent together before the White House gala Tammy turned out to be a great guide to the sights of Washington and a perceptive student of its personalities. I began to understand why as I pieced together the bits of her biography that I picked up as we talked. Her heritage was Syrian. Her mother was born in Pittsburgh, the daughter of a priest in the Antiochian Eastern Orthodox Church; her father, also a Christian, had come to this country at age eighteen with his mother to join his father, who had established a store in Washington, Pennsylvania. Talk about living the American dream! When I met Tammy, Shakir Ilyas was a physician in Munhall, a Pittsburgh suburb, an officer of the Medical Society, a national board member of the Orthodox church. In Syria the family had been so poor that Shakir's two sisters had died of starvation after the father, like so many millions of Americans before and since, had fled to this country to earn the money to save them from poverty and persecution. As Christians they often had to escape into the hills to avoid attacks by marauding Moslem neighbors. Arriving without knowing a word of English, Shakir got through high school and studied medicine at the University of Pittsburgh and Georgetown University in Washington, D.C., where his ambitious father had moved to launch two grocery stores. He served as an army doctor until he was invalided home from England after World War II with arthritis so crippling he had to switch from orthopedic surgery to general practice. But he was content, according to his daughter, and happiest when he could spend hours in his library among his books.

It was her father who had encouraged Tammy to become something of an anomaly in a family steeped in the traditions of the Old World and the church—a career woman, still unmarried at thirty-three. At that, Tammy's life was something of a compromise with family values. It would have caused too much of a breach to go on the stage as an actress or opera singer, her deep ambition. As a result she spent six years at Edinboro State College, the University of Pittsburgh and

I soon discovered that Tammy came from a remarkable family. Her father, Dr. S.T. Ilyas, was a Pittsburgh physician and a member of the Board of Directors of the Antiochian Eastern Orthodox Church of North America, the group shown here in an audience with Pope Paul (ca. 1960). Dr. and Mrs. Ilyas are at the far left next to a Vatican priest.

Duquesne University, switching from major to major in search of an alternative. Finally she accepted an associate degree and got a job as a ticket agent with United Airlines in Chicago, a job in which she could assert her independence and see something of the world. She eventually transferred with United to California for three years and then to Washington, where her sister Thelma had settled down to raise a family with her doctor husband—very much in the family tradition.

Tammy now had her eye on the job of passenger service representative. There were only twenty of these in the United system. Scattered around the most active airports, their function was to help passengers generally but to be especially helpful to the frequent-traveling VIPs so that they would choose United. It wasn't an easy job. It could call for fourteen-hour days or getting up in the middle of the night to meet a special charter flight. One day her regional manager called her in and said, "Ilyas, I don't think you can handle this job but I'll let you have it for three days." She earned enough passenger compliments in those few days to nail down the job and soon was stealing frequent fliers from other airlines. One such coup was snatching TV personality Arthur Godfrey from American. On more than a first-name basis with several of Washington's movers and shakers, Tammy was often involved in their private lives, as when Sen. Robert Dole and his first wife, Phyllis, went through their divorce. A typical Ilyas job performance would turn out to have interesting consequences for the two of us.

One day she saw a distinguished-looking gentleman in civilian clothes running down the hall with a lady in tow. She was sure that she had seen his face somewhere. He wasn't asking for help but was clearly in trouble. When she stopped the man he said, "I'm Bud Zumwalt. My sister here has lost her ticket and she has to catch a flight to Bakersfield in five minutes." All the pieces clicked in Tammy's head. This had to be Adm. Elmo Zumwalt—not only an admiral but the Chief of Naval Operations. No high-ranking officer had ever introduced himself so informally, but when she said, "Come with me, Admiral Zumwalt," he responded with a broad smile. As they ran together toward the gate, Tammy explained that she would put his sister on without a ticket and phone Bakersfield to meet her and make arrangements at that end. Before long Tammy was having tea at the Admiral's quarters, now the vice-president's home, and getting to know all of the traveling Zumwalt family.

It remains a wonder to me that I made any impression on her at all, considering the people she was meeting every day. But right after she put me on that plane to San Francisco, I would learn, she called her sister and told her, "I've just met the man I'm going to marry." Apparently that announcement was taken with several grains of salt by her family. So far no man had matched the ideal of husband and father that her own father had established in her mind. As much as she enjoyed her job, Tammy wanted above everything else to establish a family of her own, and she kept praying that she would meet a man she could live with the rest of her life. She had actually been thinking about giving up her job, going back to Pittsburgh and adopting a child as a single parent if that year of 1973 passed without an answer to her prayers. Both of us believed then, and believe now, in the power of prayer, and nothing has so reinforced that belief for both of us as the fact that Tammy apparently saw her answer in me.

Of course, I was pretty much unaware of all this in that merry month of May. I still wasn't thinking too far ahead. I was, though, aware that the chemistry between us was right, that we had felt immediately comfortable with each other and that this feeling grew with each minute together. And Tammy was as clever as she was determined. One of the arts she *hadn't* mastered was cooking. The meal she concocted at our first dinner in her apartment consisted of tacos—boiled instead of fried. It was a disaster from her point of view, although anything edible was a feast to me after so many years of prison slop. But since her sister and brother-in-law happened to be out of town, Tammy insisted on taking me on the following evenings to have dinners with their children, dinners deliciously cooked by her brother-in-law Bob's mother, who was baby-sitting.

The event of May 24, 1973, was described in the papers as the "most spectacular White House gala in history." It began in the afternoon with a speech by President Nixon to more than 600 of us POWs in the State Department auditorium. With the publication of the Pentagon Papers in mind, he defended secrecy in the interests of national defense and we gave him a standing ovation. Then he stood there on the stage for an hour shaking every hand. When I reached him, the President clasped both my hands in his, then gripped me by the shoulders.

"You look well. You look well," he said, and then added, "I want you to know that I tried . . . I really tried . . ."

"Yes, sir, I understand," I said.

Mr. Nixon's evident emotional reaction to our survival and release was underscored by what Tammy told me about the tea that Mrs. Nixon was giving upstairs at the State Department for the women while the President was meeting us. His

POWs and their ladies from all over the country were reunited for President Nixon's White House party in May, 1973. With me are Jerry Coffee, on my right, and Read McCleary, on my left. Between Jerry and me is Tammy Ilyas, my date for the evening who would become my date for life. (*UPI International News Pictures*)

daughter Tricia went out of her way to find Tammy and tell her how much my letter had meant to her father in a time of troubles. They all had wept while the President read it aloud in the family circle, she said.

In the evening there was a sit-down dinner under a huge tangerine-striped tent pitched on the White House lawn. More than 1,300 guests were assigned to one of 120 round tables. Unfortunately, it had been raining all day and the lawn was a muddy squish underfoot, but there were bright lights and music and it would have been impossible to dampen the spirit of the gathering. There was an interesting moment when Henry Kissinger, then National Security Advisor, let me know that I was famous for more than my endurance. "Ah, Alvarez," he said, "I know your mother well. She gave me a rough time." After that it was a pleasure to find John Wayne, whom I had met at the Academy Awards, at our table. He had, I swear, tears in his eyes, which he explained to Tammy in a whisper: "I have such admiration for Commander Alvarez that every time I look at him I can't help but cry."

There were no tears shed by the POWs that night. I'm sure that many others like myself had a hard time realizing that being there wasn't another of those grand hallucinations that sometimes visited us in prison. During that evening we were all able to feel that we had served a noble cause, that our and others' sacrifices had been worthwhile. But with the treatment we were receiving we couldn't really appreciate the plight of the other Vietnam veterans. For the most part they were slinking back apologetically into a society that was unfairly placing the blame for its disillusionment about the war on the men it had drafted for the fighting. It would take time before we could comprehend the extent and nature of this peculiar war's wounds, before we would feel obliged to become part of the healing process. For now we celebrated survival.

ALL WEEK a pleasant kind of tension had been building between Tammy and me. On the dance floor of Le Bateau, a floating nightclub on the Potomac, it broke. "Why don't you just admit that you love me?" Tammy asked while we were holding each other close, and I did. From then on there would be no turning back although the course of true love would be far from smooth.

Everything went, as they say, swimmingly, at first. There were no legal barriers between us since my civil divorce in the United States had come through soon after our first meeting. There were no physical barriers either, thanks to

The day after the White House gala, Tammy and I were together again and on our way to a whirlwind courtship.

Tammy's position as a valued employee of United. That vast stretch of continent that had loomed so large when I first thought about her virtually disappeared, since she could use her free passes to join me in California on weekends whenever I couldn't wrangle Navy business to join her in Washington. But even in Navy affairs Tammy's influence surpassed mine, as I soon discovered.

Much of Tammy's charm and power comes from a total disregard, as distinguished from disrespect, for rank in the military or the pecking order in civilian society. It could be mistaken for naivety, but it's really more a matter of an inbred feeling of self-worth, that she and hers are on an equal footing with anybody. One time when Admiral Zumwalt's secretary called to invite Tammy and me to join the Zum-walts for a cruise on the Potomac River in the admiral's barge, she told her, "Oh, I don't know, Carolina. Everett is pretty busy out there in California, I don't think we can come." The secretary suggested that Tammy call me anyway and give me the date, time and place that the Chief of Naval Operations had specified. "Well, I know Everett, so don't count on it." Carolina could only smile and shake her head. Tammy knew me pretty well, but she hadn't come to grips with Alvarez the Navy officer. "Well, you just tell Commander Alvarez that Admiral Zumwalt says it's an order," Carolina said. "He'll know what it means." When she had me on the phone Tammy said, "Do you know what that means?" I told her, "Absolutely. You tell him I'll be there. Period."

By June my frenzy of activity had exhausted me, and my friend Jim Shea arranged for me to become a service member of San Francisco's Bohemian Club and spend two weeks at its encampment among the California redwoods. For me it was a blissful, restful time out of time. The Bohemian Grove is a place where you might find yourself peeling potatoes for the evening meal beside a president of the United States or a president of General Motors. That summer I was able to hike the trails with one of history's great air heroes, Gen. Jimmy Doolittle, and canoe through the rapids of the Russian River with magazine writer Robert O'Brien. No women were allowed in the Grove. There are no phones in the camps, discouraging all but emergency communication with the outside world. Yet I kept getting Tammy's message as one after another of the men I met took me aside and said, "I hear you're seeing Tammy Ilyas. Wonderful girl!"

There was a different kind of reaction to my romance in Santa Clara, Salinas and points south as I introduced Tammy to my family. She was not only from the East but she wasn't Mexican or even Roman Catholic. When her frequent flying out to California to be with me made it clear she wasn't just another date, she was perceived as a threat. My family and I hadn't yet bridged the gap between us, and Tammy in my life could make that gap even wider. Oh, there was no overt hostility. My mother reacted with the correct behavior and tight-lipped silence that had seen her through a lifetime of difficult relationships. Tammy, extremely sensitive to the chill atmosphere, did her best to warm things up, as in her own demonstrative family, and for her trouble earned the rather derisive nickname, "the kisser." Her best efforts weren't very successful, and I retreated behind that Plexiglas emotional shield I'd fashioned for myself.

The religious issue was much tougher for me to handle. It came up in late summer after Tammy and I had agreed that we would marry. Once I had my divorce, I confidently applied to the San Francisco diocese for an annulment of my first marriage. One good result of my publicity, I felt, was that Tangee's leaving me for another man while I was in captivity was at least a matter of public record. So was the honor and friendship I received from the priestly fellowship at Santa Clara University. That I wasn't a Johnny-come-lately to the church or a foxhole Christian had had national notice even before my release when Father Michael Buckley, my parish priest in Salinas, told Morley Safer on "60 Minutes" that I had been a "very sincere, very conscientious" altar boy. I didn't think it was necessary to indulge in any special pleading for my case, and my reluctance then to discuss details of my imprisonment extended to the role that my faith had played in my survival. I had found myself literally saying the Lord's Prayer when I hit the water after ejecting, and on the very first Sunday I spent in the Hanoi Hilton I had used a rusty nail to scratch the outline of a cross into the stone wall beside my cell door to create a crude altar. From then on, prayer had been a daily companion, and I had regularly reconstructed as much of the mass in Latin as I could remember to worship at my altar.

It was a shock akin to being shot down when I got a letter from a Monsignor Knapp, representing Archbishop Joseph McGucken, with the news that they had contacted Tangee, discovered that she, like I, had entered into our marriage with the intention of maintaining a lifelong union and bearing children, and reached the conclusion that an annulment could not be granted. "It is indeed unfortunate that you should be the one called upon to suffer in this situation, since it would seem that you are totally the innocent party in the breakup of the marriage," the letter said in part. "However, our office can do no more than point out that our investigation shows no real grounds for challenging the validity of that marriage according to the norms of church law. . . . Please be assured of my continued prayers for your acceptance of this unfortunate situation." I knew what this meant. If I remarried I would be denied the sacraments, a deeply spiritual part of worship that had always meant much to me even when dispensed by a French-speaking Vietnamese priest approved by our Communist jailors. I would, in effect, be outside the pale of the church that had proved so sustaining in my long years as a captive. It was a deeply troubling thought.

The timing of the letter couldn't have been worse. It arrived just before I was heading east to keep an important date with Tammy. Another of our VIP cupids, Ron Walker, head of the Park Service under Nixon, had given Tammy tickets for the Bolshoi Ballet at the Wolftrap summer festival outside Washington. Knowing Tammy's love for music and dance, I managed to keep the bad news to myself for the first half of the program. But it was bursting inside me, and at intermission, as we stood by the refreshment stand, I told her, "I think we have a real problem. The church won't give me an annulment." Tammy's temper flared. "How can you say that? The Catholic church isn't God!" And I knew she was not speaking lightly. She was as devoted to her church as I was to mine, as much a believer in God as I was.

"I know what you mean," I told her. "The church is made up of men, and men can change their minds. I can't get mad at the church because of what a few individuals are doing to me. It's meant too much to me. I don't think I would be alive without it. Let's see what we can do."

Aware of how deeply I felt, Tammy agreed to explore some avenues in Washington while I worked through San Francisco. But her well-meaning effort only made things worse. The neighborhood Catholic priest she consulted advised her that the only solution was for us to live together out of wedlock. "It would kill my mother," she told him, and stomped out. Back in California, Governor Reagan, Congressman Talcott, and Mayor Alioto of San Francisco wrote to the Archbishop on my behalf—and got nowhere. My Jesuit friends at Santa Clara said that they didn't agree with the ruling and suggested I try another diocese. I refused to shop around. I didn't think it was necessary or right for me to do that. After all, the fault wasn't mine. Father Schmidt, a man who had come to the Catholic faith from a Jewish background, was the one who came to my rescue. When Tammy said that her Eastern Orthodox church would sanctify our marriage, Father Schmidt assured me that God would, too. Beyond that, he promised to give me the sacraments personally whenever I could get to Santa Clara, and he kept that promise until the day he died. Tammy's church proved to have its limitations, too. Although the Eastern Orthodox church had permitted our marriage, it wouldn't let me take communion. We have since solved the problem in our own way. We go to Tammy's church for regular services, and our sons have been baptized in that faith. Occasionally Tammy and I take communion together in a Catholic church where the priest evidently shares Father Schmidt's views. We find God in both places.

Once the religious issue was settled, we were on the high road to romance again. The wedding that Tammy's parents staged in Pittsburgh on October 27, 1973, was only a little less splendid—and far more important for us—than the White House gala. There was an elaborate ritual in St. George's Orthodox Church, enhanced by my uniformed POW friends, who showed up to make an arch of swords for us. Strings from the Pittsburgh Symphony played at dinner and for dancing afterward at the Allegheny Club at the city's Three Rivers Stadium complex. With some persuasion and financial help, my parents got together one more time to come from California along with Madeleine and her new husband; Delia was in Europe. It wasn't a perfect blending of families, by any means. I could sense that my family thought that I was slipping off again into an alien world before I had really returned to theirs. But I didn't let that feeling spoil the day for me or for Tammy. I felt we were entitled to the kind of happiness that the great event was promising.

On October 27, 1973, the Ilyas family staged a wedding as splendid as the White House gala. Seven former Hanoi Hilton cellmates participated.

Charlie Zuhoski is straightening Chuck Rice's tie before the big event as I watch.

The beginning of "happily ever after."

DURING THE MONTHS that we had spent straightening out the religious matter, I had also made a decision about my immediate professional future. I had been selected for the Navy's postgraduate school at Monterey, California, before I was shot down, and I now reapplied for that. But first I wanted to get back into the cockpit, to let freedom in the air blow the dust of my confinement out of my system, to live a little of the carefree youth I had lost. I signed on for retraining in Kingsville, Texas, where I knew that many of my fellow POWs would also be stationed. There, hidden away in the ranks of the Navy, I could get off the celebrity stage and concentrate on a private life with Tammy. So after the wedding we packed up and headed south and west with high hopes and light hearts.

CHAPTER IV

The Wrong Side of the Tracks

THE HIGH THAT Tammy and I were on when leaving for Texas was in stark contrast to some other times in my life. The worst part of falling into enemy hands in time of war is the feeling of losing control over your life. Minute to minute, night or day, you never know when they will come for you or what they will do to you. This was particularly true in North Vietnam. The enemy's culture, values and political system were so different from my own that I couldn't even guess about his intentions. I had to accept and make the most of whatever came along. Fortunately for me, my whole life up to the point of being shot down had been a training in this process. There are no guarantees or certainties, only challenges and opportunities. Although I wasn't aware of it until I faced the uncontrollable circumstances of imprisonment, I had learned that the only thing I could control was myself— and that, if I did my best, I could leave the rest up to God.

Survival wasn't easy in Salinas, California, when I was born on December 23, 1937. My birth itself was hard; the doctor had to haul me out with forceps. But my mother had high hopes for me from the start because of a strange occurrence that she took more literally than I would have. While she was outside the hospital in a wheelchair with me in her arms, waiting for my father to bring the car around, a man all dressed in black said, "What a pretty baby. May I feel his head?" Mother said "Sure" and the man ran his hands lightly over my head. "This baby's head has the shape of a famous person," he told her, and wandered off. No harm done, I suppose, except to give her great expectations.

They took me home to a one-room and kitchen apartment above a garage. Both my mother, Soledad Rivera, and my father, Everett Alvarez, Sr., had to drop out of grade school to help with family finances by taking on any available work. When I came along Dad was barely twenty and Mother eighteen. They had a place to take me mostly because of inverse luck. Just before their marriage they and my mother's mother, Simona, whom we always called MaMona, were victims of an automobile accident. MaMona used a $1,700 settlement to buy a property in Salinas with a small house and the garage apartment; my father used a $500 settlement to buy the car that took them on their honeymoon.

More than a honeymoon, it was a trip to southern California to visit relatives in the hopes of finding a better job for Dad. At the time he was working in a warehouse heaving 120-pound sacks all day and was suffering from stomach trouble that dropped his weight from 144 to 129 pounds. Attributing his condition to a combination of physical strain and dust in the air, he quit the job not long after I was born, took a correspondence course in carpentry and helped some relatives build a house, thereby learning his first trade and acquiring a respect for the power of education. But there was no money in building. Despite not being able to shake his mysterious illness, he signed on with the "bull gang" at the Spreckels Sugar Company, where beets were refined into sugar. Dad's duties involved stepping into any laboring job in place of any man who didn't show up for work. When the season ended in December and the men were laid off, Dad checked himself into county hospital, where he was diagnosed as suffering from chronic appendicitis that was finally relieved by an appendectomy. After that he played catch-as-catch-can with jobs until another bit of strange luck intervened. When war broke out Dad went to San Francisco to look for opportunities. He saw a sign advertising a two-week welding course for $125. On the Monday after he finished the course he signed up with Bethlehem Pipe & Steel Co. to weld high-pressure lines in the ships Bethlehem was building for the war effort. He had gotten another trade through education, and the Alvarez family began to have a future.

On $1.35 an hour Dad was able to bring Mother and me and baby Delia up to San Francisco. It was 1942, and I was four going on five, old enough to start storing up the first retrievable memories. We lived in the Mission District in a cluster of single-family houses, each with a backyard where a kid could play. There were caves to explore on the slope behind the city hospital on Russian Hill a block away and a stream full of tadpoles running through the scrap yard at the foot of the hill. I went through the first three grades of school there, and I can remember liking it well enough to bring home good marks. But when I brought home from the school a friend who wasn't a neighbor to play with me I got my first lesson in the law of gangs. The other boys on the block chased him away, and I, as the smallest of them, couldn't defend him. As something of outsiders, Delia and I were thrown together. I often played—and sometimes fought—with her even though she was three years younger. It was not exactly an idyllic time, but I remember a freedom in those San Francisco days that wouldn't be possible today. A gang of seven- or eight-year-olds thought nothing of hopping a cable car for a ride down to the center of town. On Saturday afternoons my mother would press change into my fist and let me walk eight blocks to the nearest movie house by myself. For a summer break she would put me on a bus alone to ride the hundred miles to Salinas, where I would then take a taxi to my grandmother's house.

As with many men in that blue collar community, my father sought relief from days of hard labor by drinking with the men he knew at work or met in bars. It must have meant long, lonely nights and weekends for my mother, who was separated from her mother and friends in Salinas. It must also have put a strain on a necessarily tight budget that was

her job to manage. Whatever the causes, the differences between my parents got to a point in 1947 that prompted my
mother to take Delia and me back to Salinas to live in a small
rented house that my grandmother had acquired next to her
own. For me, it was a double disaster. I had the trauma of
transferring to a new school. It was January and I had just
started third grade in San Francisco. Although they let me
stay in the Salinas third grade that would finish in spring,
they put me with the slow learners. The other disaster was
being separated from my father, whose masculine presence
filled the house when he was home.

I don't know whether I communicated these feelings to my
mother or not, but when school was out in the summer of
1947 she sent me up to visit her sister Cecelia and her husband Al Sanchez, who were living in San Francisco then with
their two boys Danny and Al, Jr., and daughter Linda. As soon
as I got there I went looking for my father. Nobody seemed to
know where he was living but we knew where he worked.
He'd had another lean time of it. He and some five thousand
others in the Boilermakers Union had been thrown out of
work on the ships by a machinists' strike right after V-E Day
in 1945. Again he had used some of his idle time to go to the
Samuel Gompers Trade School to learn how to lay out pat-
terns before he landed a new job in a shop making trailers. It
was fifteen blocks from the Sanchez house but I walked it and
arrived at quitting time. I hung around the gate asking each
departing worker for Everett Alvarez until *he* finally appeared. I can't, of course, remember all that we said to each
other, but at one point I asked if he could take me to the
movies. He said yes and that he'd pick me up at my uncle's
the next night.

I walked on air all the way back. The next night Uncle Al
took my cousins to another movie because I was going out
with my dad. I waited and I waited and he never came. I was
only nine, and I was devastated. I really cried hard that night.
My Aunt Cecelia must have passed the word to my mother,
because she came up the next day on the bus and went to see
Dad. When she came back she said, "Your father didn't come

for you because he didn't have the money. I'll take you to the movies tonight." Whether that incident had anything to do with it or not, Dad came down to Salinas at the end of the summer, got a job in a sheeting, plumbing and heating place where he could finish the training he had started in San Francisco at night, and we were once again a family.

In those days Salinas was a town divided—literally and as in song and story—by the tracks of the Southern Pacific Railroad. Everything east of the tracks out toward the airport was called "little Oklahoma" because it had been settled by the migrant workers from the Dust Bowl of the thirties. Although there were very few blacks, the neighborhood was otherwise a mixed bag ethnically and racially. The Mexican migrant workers lived in camps further out, and the businessmen, farm owners, professional people—Anglos for the most part—lived on the west side of the tracks. But in those grade-school years we didn't know that we were on the wrong side of the tracks. Important to me on our side of town was the conversion of the barracks of a wartime air base into civilian housing. When they finally moved me out of the slow learners and into fifth grade I got to know a classmate from the development named Joe Kapp. His father, a traveling salesman of pots and pans, had served in the Army in California and had recently moved Joe and the rest of the family up from New Mexico. It was a case of instant friendship that has lasted a lifetime.

Joe and I shared everything—work and worship as well as play. Living only five blocks apart, we could ride our bicycles back and forth. For both of us work was just a fact of life. Mother got me started when Dad was in San Francisco. Around home my responsibility was to tend the garden we had in the yard; during spring vacation she asked my uncle Philip, a foreman on a ranch outside Salinas, to take me with him and his sons to the fields. "Don't pay him," she told Uncle Philip. "Just teach him to work." My mother or grandmother would rise before sunup, pack me a lunch and send me off in the dark to walk the block and a half to Uncle Philip's house. There I would sit down with my uncle and his sons, men in their early twenties, to a breakfast of scrambled eggs, home fries, beans, tortillas. Wonderfully full, we would ride through the dawn on Uncle Philip's flatbed truck to the ranch, which consisted of fifteen acres of truck farm products like carrots and tomatoes. I would help older boys lugging sections of irrigation pipe from one place to another or hoeing the rows between plants. I liked the adventure of it, liked being outdoors, and at the end of the week Uncle Philip would slip me fifty cents in spite of what my mother said. For the next three or four years I kept at this kind of work in vacation times, with Joe often joining me.

What money I earned I gave to my mother. She would dole it out for occasional fun but keep most of it for my school clothing—one pair of good jeans and a couple of sweaters. Sharing earnings within the family was just something that was expected. In Joe's case it was even more needed than in mine. His mother helped to keep bread on the table by working as a waitress, which meant that Joe often had to baby-sit with the younger children. If going into the fields taught us at a very young age that you have to work for anything you get, as our mothers hoped it would, it also taught us that doing stooped labor from sunup to sundown was no way to live. Both of us decided that we would become sailors or welders or just about anything else when we grew up.

There wasn't much idle time in our lives. At 7:00 A.M. on Sundays, Joe and I would be at St. Mary's of the Nativity Church to serve as altar boys. My parents didn't always go, and I would often take Delia with me on the handlebar of my bike. Even then she was questioning authority. Once when Father Buckley reprimanded her for some mistake she had made in the order of confession she ran crying out to Dad, who had come that day to pick us up in the car. Quick-tempered like Delia, Dad jumped out and was heading into the church to give the priest hell when I managed to calm him down. It was only one of the many times when I would act as the Alvarez peacekeeper. What time Joe and I could steal for ourselves we devoted to sports. We didn't have much in the way of facilities. We had to walk clear across town to use the municipal swimming pool; there was no Little League in our neighborhood; the only sport in the new junior high school that they were actually building grade by grade as we went through it was basketball. When they finally built the ninth grade there was a gym, which I mostly appreciated for the showers I could take.

A shower wasn't the only thing missing in the little house on my grandmother's Pearl Street property. Delia and I shared a bedroom so small that we had to use bunk beds. Being older and a boy, I had the upper bunk. It was an enforced togetherness that, in our case, made us much closer than most brothers and sisters. When I was in eighth grade my father was doing well enough that he could rent a house on Alisal Street across from the airport, a location that would determine the whole thrust of my life. My parents got to know Fergie, a World War II pilot who had turned mechanic and was taking care of a fleet of a dozen biwinged Stearman crop-dusters. With Fergie's permission I would go over and climb into the cockpit of one of the old planes and work the stick and rudder pedals while I imagined myself one of the daring fighter pilots I saw in the movies. On one glorious day Fergie offered to take me up. I was in the back cockpit, clinging like grim death to the rails as we taxied and lifted off. Once in the air, Fergie turned around, smiled and said, "Relax, kid. Enjoy the view!" Seeing him nonchalantly smoking a cigarette, I did relax and peer over the side. I'll never forget watching the city below dwindle into a toy town. Then and there, being a pilot became my impossible dream.

THE FIRST TIME I was really conscious of living on the wrong side of the tracks was when Joe and I and a few others accepted an invitation to a mixer at the Washington Junior High School on the west side. We rode over on our bikes through a neighborhood that had sidewalks instead of gutters and larger homes than little Oklahoma. At the dance we stood along the wall and ogled the "rich" girls. Although nothing was said, we had the feeling that we might make trouble if we asked them to dance. I think it was more an economic than an ethnic or racial thing. Being Mexican—Joe's mother was Mexican—wasn't something we really thought about then. Looking back on it, when we were growing up in Salinas it was an ethnic mixed bag. The farm area had a lot of Scandinavians and Italians besides Mexicans. It wasn't polarized. My so-called gang in those days was made up of jocks, the guys in sports. We hung around together and wore the same jackets because they were team jackets.

Football was *the* fall sport, and Joe and I were out there on the first afternoon for practice. Neither of us weighed as much as 130 pounds, and we were tried out as ends on the last team. Most of our time we spent picking ourselves up off the ground. Without Joe's example I'm not sure that I would have stuck it out. Because he was already getting the height that would allow him to carry the weight he would need one day to become a pro, Joe was awkward and gawky and always being kidded. But he hung in there, and by the end of the season he was getting a chance to play in more games than I was. Perseverance—or something he would later call "fire in the heart"—was Joe's secret. He kept practicing, practicing, trying, trying. It was no accident that Joe made the basketball team that first winter in high school when I didn't, and the lesson wasn't lost on me. I would take it with me in the spring when we split—he to the baseball field, I to the track. We would watch each other work out, cheer each other on. It was a real blow when Joe's family moved to Los Angeles at the end of that school year.

But by then I was blending in with the west-side students in academics as well as sports. Nobody in the Alvarez or Sanchez families had ever thought of going to college, and it wasn't on my mind when I entered high school. I was assigned to the noncollege track that included things like shop courses that I found a waste of time. The kids I was playing football and running with from Washington Junior High were taking the college prep-curriculum. I asked to switch because I liked math and science and English and history and felt I could compete in these studies. When I told Dad about it he said, "Well, why not go to college then?" Family finances were no secret to me. "Where would I get the money?" He said, "You do the studying, and we'll find a way."

That was typical of Dad, and my mother was equally supportive. They were always encouraging me, and there always did seem to be a way. For instance, I was the only boy in my scout troop with a full uniform even though we didn't have any more money than the others. They came to watch me play football, and when he could afford it Dad took me to see a few big college and pro games. My parents really believed in learning, and they did more than preach it. Aside from attending courses to improve his work skills, Dad was always reading the newspapers, and Mom got to be a history buff. In the good family times when they would pile us kids into the car for a Sunday drive, often as not the destination was one of the old mission churches Mom had been reading about. On one of those drives through the valley Mother pointed to the Japanese working the fields. "Look at them," she said. "The Mexicans are hung over from Saturday night. The Japanese are out there working to send their kids through school." They never pushed; they pulled.

Just the possibility of going on to college was incentive enough, not only for studying but for working. No matter what Dad said, the money wasn't there, and we all knew that it wouldn't grow on trees or out on the farm fields. Dad had been doing his best to make us better off. When Madeleine was born in 1952, he took a gamble and signed on for a short-term, well-paying job on a construction project in Alaska. The money he earned he put into a lot on Williams Road, a better location than the rental across from the airport, and he stayed out of work to build the house himself. It had three bedrooms, and for the first time in my life I had a room to myself. Although Dad got a job again in the maintenance department of Kaiser Aluminum, I decided that I needed work that would be steadier than picking fruit or hoeing vegetables. I found a job as dishwasher at a Lucky store soda fountain and lunch counter in the summer after I finished tenth grade. It paid $1.15 an hour. I worked double shift six days a week, riding back and forth five miles each way on my bike. It was a good job because I was able to hang onto it right through high school, working night shift when school was in session so that I could keep up with my athletics.

If I ever felt deprived or somehow demeaned by the amount and kind of work I had to do, the feeling hasn't stuck with me. At that time and in that place it was a necessary way of life, and it was the only way up and out. Although I probably wasn't aware of it at the time, I was also learning a kind of fierce independence from my father's example. Unstable as his work career might seem, his willingness to do almost anything and to learn new techniques enabled him to survive and improve. He depended on himself, not circumstances. He didn't believe in getting trapped, in meekly accepting unfairness and injustice. He let me know that I should have the same attitude on the very first night of my dishwashing job.

A nasty part of the work at Lucky was mopping up in front at closing time. After my first double shift I was tired and the buckets were very big. I wasn't moving very fast, I guess, but doing as well as I could when the store manager came out screaming at me, "Get a move on, kid! You're doing it all wrong. You're too damned slow." For him it was the end of a long day, he wanted to lock up and go home. I was too young to understand that. I thought that I was a failure, sure to lose my job. How would I tell my parents? Misery grew with every push of the pedals on the ride home. All I wanted to do was sneak into my bed and cry. But Dad was there to greet me, and he could read my feelings in my face. When I blurted out the story he said, "You don't have to take that, Junior. You go back there tomorrow and tell him you're a young guy. You're learning. You're trying. If he doesn't like it, you quit." The sanction to quit gave me the courage to go back. The woman who ran the fountain area told me, "Don't pay any attention to him. He's always grouchy at the end of the day." The manager never stopped complaining, but I got good enough to train other dishwashers.

In contrast to my father, my mother and MaMona were studies in stoicism and perseverance. Thanks to their management of whatever we had, there was always a roof overhead, food on the table, clothes that were mended and clean on our backs. There was a good deal of Indian blood, probably Aztec, in both of these women, and it showed in their dark skins and lean, sinewy frames, as well as in their quiet endurance. MaMona had been born in a Mexican village, married at thirteen to an adventurous sixteen-year-old who took off to work on the railways in California, returning periodically to sire a family. Eventually MaMona joined him in a nomadic life along the rail lines. She bore twelve children of whom only my mother, the eleventh, an older sister, Cecelia, and a much older brother, Joe, survived. MaMona was widowed when mother was only four. The family existed on Joe's earnings from on-again-off-again jobs and what MaMona and the girls could pick in the fields. A remarriage wasn't helpful. Her husband returned to Mexico, and MaMona wanted the promise of America for her children. Life had more or less stabilized for her in Salinas with the marriages of her daughters to hard-working men, but she had to absorb one more blow: Joe turned into a mentally disturbed man who would end his days in the psychiatric ward of a veterans hospital.

We Alvarez kids and our Sanchez cousins would have to be the ones to reach that promised land that MaMona glimpsed. So she and my mother were back of me in every upward step I took. In the Mexican-American tradition for women they stayed close to home, living vicariously through us children. They were not only interested in what we were doing but also in what we were thinking. Mother, for instance, would often gobble up the books I started bringing home in junior high. So would Delia. Although we no longer shared a room, my sister and I stayed involved with each other. I would help her with her homework; she was thinking about college a lot earlier than I had. For a Mexican-American girl to have such aspirations was close to revolutionary; yet MaMona and mother encouraged her, too. As willing to work as I was, Delia got a job clerking in a supermarket as soon as she was old enough. In the unfairness of things, she only earned a dollar an hour compared to my $1.15. But we were both savers and got into the habit of exchanging loans that would play an important part in both of our lives.

In the domestic turmoil of the household, Delia and I were natural allies. We loved both of our parents for different reasons and in different ways. Dad would wrestle with me on the floor to teach me that boys can take physical pain without crying, and he would use his strength and temper in defense of Delia to give her a sense of masculine protection. Until we were twelve or so we were a little afraid of Dad, but then we were proud of him because other adults were afraid of him too. Mother was the indispensable presence, the source of life in every way. When our parents fought, it was frightening and we reacted according to our natures. More emotional than I, Delia would literally throw herself between them; I would try to pick up the pieces.

I had too much of a load to carry in school and at work to let these family matters get to me. Beginning with the rental in Alisal Street, where I had to sleep and study in a corner of the living room, I developed the fine art of withdrawal. I know that my ability to keep calm and concentrate often drove Delia up the wall, but I couldn't have managed otherwise.

By the time I got to be a senior in high school I thought I was in clover. Setting my sights on the University of California at Berkeley because Dad had once taken me to a football game there, I was doing well with the kind of courses that challenged me—physics, calculus, English, history. I was a starter on the lightweight football team. I had a driver's license, and Dad was generous with the car if I had a date, not that I had many. My social circles were entirely on the west side of the tracks, and it came to my ears that a beauty, daughter of a Scandinavian who was a successful building contractor, wanted to go out with me. The contact came through a girlfriend of hers and a boyfriend of mine, and we started to double date, meeting at her friend's house. We hit it off well, and the time came when we wanted to be alone together, a desire that led to one of the surprises of my young life.

I can remember feeling confident and full of interesting romantic plans when I parked Dad's car at the curb and walked up to her house to meet her parents and take her out.

Her parents looked me over rather coolly, I thought, and when we were alone together in the car she told me that her father had ruled that this would be our one and only date. "Why?" In tears she said, "Because you're Mexican. It doesn't matter to me. We can meet secretly, at my girlfriend's house or something." I told her that wouldn't be right and drove home thoroughly crushed. The minute I walked into the house, my mother sensed my mood. She asked my father to find out what was wrong. When he wormed the story out of me, he wasn't angry for a change; he was gentle, even meditative.

"Look, Junior," he said, "don't let it bother you. You *can't* let it bother you. This may be the first time you've run into something like this, but it won't be the last. You're a good boy. You're clean. You're not a bum. You're a hard worker. That fellow—you know what he is?—he's ignorant. You're better than they are."

That's the way Dad handled me in every serious crisis—"Chin up. *You're* OK so you'll *be* OK." Thinking over his words that night, I went through an epiphany of sorts. I saw clearly that there was nothing I could ever do about being of Mexican descent. Inside, I knew who I was, why I was, what I could do. I had a right to be as proud of my Spanish/Indian/Mexican background as other Americans were of their different heritages. As a good scholar and athlete I also had a right to dream the American dream. Others couldn't know this just by looking at me. If they misjudged me by my skin color or the spelling of my name, it *was* a form of ignorance, and *they* were the poorer for it.

Whether because of blighted romance, overwork or adolescence, I wasn't doing well in track as the season opened. Younger kids were beating my times so consistently that Coach Bill Kearney finally told me that he'd have to keep me out of the meets. From the way he said it I knew that I was letting him down badly, and Coach Kearney wasn't the kind of guy you wanted to let down. He would take time to work with each of us, give us rubdowns, pep talks. I admired him as a man, he had values. I'd been improving with his guidance each year, and he had been counting on me to give the school a name in middle-distance running. Of course, I would be letting myself down, too—and my old friend Joe Kapp. Joe and I had kept in touch, and he had been doing so well in sports that he was already accepted at Cal on a full football scholarship. What would Joe think of me? With Joe on my mind I tried to light that fire in my heart by working harder, staying later for practice, running more laps. It worked, and I ended up representing Salinas in the Northern California State Meet. Turning myself around on the track brought the unexpected reward of Coach Kearney making me a counselor at the camp for underprivileged children that he and his wife ran up in the mountains. The pay wasn't great, but I had always liked being outdoors and had never had anything like a vacation.

It's hard to overestimate the influence on my life of Kearney's faith in me. He promoted growth by giving me responsibilities. He wanted to see me succeed at Cal, where he had gone, and we often talked about it when we sat around in evening bull sessions with the coach and Mrs. Kearney, a former army nurse. As far as I was concerned, everything was set. Mother had helped solve the family financial problem by going to work in the packing sheds, and MaMona had stepped into the breach to take care of Madeleine while mother was away. My application, accompanied by good grades and good recommendations, had been filed with the university in good order. An acceptance should arrive any day. When Dad and Mother drove up to the camp one Sunday, I was sure that it had come. But the expression on their faces told the story even before they got out of the car.

I had applied for the engineering school because I was good in math and because an engineering degree offered the best chance at a good job. In turning me down the Cal admissions office did strongly suggest that I would eventually get in if I attended a junior college first. A great many of my classmates were planning to attend Hartnell Junior College. To me, going there seemed like a rejection, except for the Kearneys. The coach said, "Hey, that's great, Everett. You're sure to get in if you do a couple of years at Hartnell." His wife took me aside and said something that my parents could never have said: "Think of your parents, Everett. They can save so much while you live at home and go to Hartnell that sending you to Cal won't be as much of a strain on them."

It was a pleasant surprise to discover that about two-thirds of the engineering class at Hartnell were older men, Korean War veterans, many of them married. They were serious people, which made for a good atmosphere for learning. I was elected Associated Student Body Men's Representative, which, frankly, meant mostly working with the women's representative to plan the events of Sadie Hawkins Day, an annual blowout of games, contests, dinner and dance. Not too heavy.

My second year at Hartnell I applied for the upper division in electrical engineering at Cal and took the admissions examination. I picked electrical engineering because it was hardest to get into—and the graduates commanded the highest salaries. A professor told me I wasn't the electrical engineering *type* because I was into sports and other extracurricular activities instead of playing around with gadgets in the labs all of the time. Being cautious, I decided to cover myself by applying to another school—Santa Clara University, a private school with a higher tuition than Cal. My parents, ever supportive, told me not to let that stand in my way. In late spring, when no responses to our applications had come through from anywhere, a group of us piled into a car and drove up to Santa Clara, and a girl in the admissions office found all of our names on a list of those accepted—the letters were just about to go out. Great news, but I still wanted to go to Cal, where Joe was. I had gone up to stay with him for a week in late summer when he reported for football practice and had fallen for the locker room ambience. But the letter from Cal said that I could be admitted to any engineering school other than electrical. This time, I turned *them* down. I would go where they really wanted me. My parents were happy about the decision in spite of the greater financial burden—there would be no coeds to distract me in my pursuit of knowledge. They did know me.

I was nineteen that summer of 1957, time to become a man about money. At my best job—driving the school bus—I had been getting $1.50 an hour; union laborers were earning $2.75. Dad discovered that I could go down and hang around the union hiring hall and pay the union dues out of my earnings if they found something for me. It meant getting up before dawn, taking my brown bag of lunch and getting there at 6:30 to wait, and wait, and wait. Finally, my name did come up and I was assigned to a gang moving furniture into a new motel. After another few days in the line they sent me out to the Kaiser Permanente dolomite quarry, where Dad was a maintenance man. The dolomite went through kilns periodically shut down to replace the fire brick. When I told Dad the name of the man I was reporting to, he said, "They're going to put you in a kiln. Watch the heat there, you'll sweat like hell. Better take a couple of salt tablets." I alternated between lugging bricks and vomiting. The next job turned out to be roofing a tall warehouse with layers of styrofoam insulation, a job that remained unfinished when the building was engulfed in a fire so hot that it melted the steel. But the beauty of being in a rolling labor pool was that something usually turned up—and this time there was a promise of real money. I was sent out with a pick-and-shovel gang to where they were widening a highway from two to four lanes about thirty miles south of Salinas. Since they wanted it done in a hurry I could work seven days a week from sunup to sundown with double time on Sundays.

This was a job worth holding onto, and I went at it full out when we were ordered to unload steel rails from a railway car. It was boiling hot, and the other men, most of them older than I, started flagging. Watching us, the foreman said, "The rest of you guys ought to work like Junior there." It didn't exactly make me popular, and several of the men simply walked off the job at the lunch break. They were not only older but wiser than I was. They knew it was a job that called for cranes, and sure enough cranes showed up the next day to finish it. But my performance had apparently led the foreman to assign me to the relatively easy job of operating a hydraulic machine to pull spikes out of rails that had already been laid. When the road work was done I finished out the summer back at the Kaiser Permanente quarry, where trucks dumped the dolomite into vats with various sized screens to sort out the rocks, and my job was keeping the screens clean on the four to midnight swing shift.

What I remember most about that job was the beauty of looking out over the lights of the valley and city below me, as if I were in flight. It seemed everything came down to—or rose up to—the hunger to fly.

The labor of the summer made me realize how lucky I was to have parents insistent on seeing me, literally, make the grades; I was determined to at least give them my best. When I saw other people my age settling for less, I was grateful for having the right parents on the wrong side of the tracks rather than the other way around.

CHAPTER V

Up, Up and Away

SANTA CLARA WAS only about fifty miles north of Salinas, but I discovered that it was intellectually and socially light-years away when I entered the university as a junior in the fall of 1957. I had a room in a boarding house run by the wife of a professor of music, and there were two premed students and two philosophy majors in other rooms. We all had meals together, and dinner talk ranged through philosophy, religion, politics, art. One premed major, Pierre Renault, seemed to me the very model of the sophisticated scholar. He had actually been to Paris. After dinner he would often invite me to his room, where he would smoke a pipe and sip wine while we talked philosophy and mathematics. The next semester I moved into another house with fellow engineering students, but those early bull sessions were not just enriching, they came in very handy years later in the Hanoi Hilton.

I had little trouble with the academic program for electrical engineering at Santa Clara, but life was another matter. I would wear a light jacket with dark stripes and dark slacks to an affair where all the other men were in dark suits. Well, I'd bought the jacket for my graduation from Hartnell and it was the only one I owned. On a dinner date in a restaurant I would likely as not pick up the wrong utensil, and my manners with women were less than de rigueur. One time when a fellow in our boarding house offered to take me to the bus station we stopped at his home en route and were sitting in the living room when his mother walked in. I just looked up and said, "Hello." He got red-faced. "Don't you . . . ? Don't you . . . ?" he started to ask, but his mother whispered something to him and he just jumped up and said, "Come on, I'll take you to the bus." He was quiet all the way and still curt with me when I got back to school. It may sound minor, but it surely wasn't at the time.

Not surprisingly, the Alvarez financial planning went awry not long after I entered Santa Clara. Dad's union went out on strike, and while he tried to wait it out I got a job in a cannery at night offloading crates of fruit from railway cars onto a conveyer belt. Finally Dad gave up on the strike and found a new job at FMC Food Machinery Corporation in San Jose adjacent to Santa Clara. Mother then decided that it would make sense to move the whole family near enough my school and Dad's work for us both to live at home and commute to save money. Mother and I together found a house in a neighborhood near a park, where she still lives. I got a scholarship that along with work and savings from living at home made it possible for Mother to be a homemaker for us again. Because Delia wanted to finish the year at Salinas High she stayed with my aunt Cecelia while my cousin Al moved in with us to go to junior college in San Jose. But senior year I still found myself $300 short for tuition and was wondering what to do about it when Delia said, "I'll loan it to you." It was a lot of money to come out of her dollar-an hour savings, and I was touched. I was even more touched when Delia would sometimes slip me a few dollars to help me out on a date.

My cousin Al Sanchez tells people I was too serious, too sober during the time he was with us in Santa Clara. Maybe I was, but I wasn't aware of it. Keeping my nose in the books or staying long in the labs was more than a matter of making sure that the family sacrifices paid off. I really enjoyed the challenges of study, I had fun with them. Even Al was impressed when I demonstrated my skill with the university's computer by making it play "The Star Spangled Banner" for him. I entered papers in contests run by the American Institute of Electrical Engineers and the Institute of Radio Engineers, and came in second behind a Stanford student in one for the Bay Area and second again in one in Seattle covering entrants from universities in eleven Western states. Those along with being third in my class in the engineering school brought job offers in my senior year from such companies as Boeing, Motorola and RCA. Yes, it all seemed to be working out as planned, except for what was going on inside my head.

The closer I got to graduation the less certain I was that I really wanted to be an engineer. My doubts could have started with the kidding I got from Al. "If you don't look out, Ev, you're going to become an engineer sitting in a corner somewhere with a little green eyeshade," he once said. "Why don't you do something exciting? Be a cop or a fireman or a jet pilot." *Jet pilot?* Strange he mentioned that, I thought at the time. I hadn't even dared to share with anybody that crazy dream of flying that had stayed with me since the little hop in a crop-duster. About the same time, Jack Purl, my Santa Clara roommate in my junior year who had already graduated and gone into the Navy's flight training program, wrote letters to me full of great stories. The clincher was my first real flight when RCA paid my way to fly east for interviews, and the exhilaration of drifting across the continent above the clouds drove *all* other options out of my mind.

BACK IN SANTA CLARA I sent in my application to the Navy and then faced the prospect of breaking the news to my parents. For them, it couldn't be good news. Quite apart from the element of risk involved in military service, joining the Navy would be a disaster financially—a starting salary of $520 a month in industry compared to $72.42 during training and a maximum of $312, including flight pay, which I didn't know about. But I was so excited about flying that I would have paid them to take me. Mother reacted with a silent stoicism that nonetheless spoke her disappointment. Dad said bluntly, "So you've spent all this time going to college just to join the Navy?"

"That isn't it, Dad," I said. "I want to be a pilot."

"Oh, a pilot? Well, that's not so bad. When you get out you could get a job with one of the big airlines—"

"That's like driving a truck. I want to fly jet fighters," I said, and then I tried to sound reasonable by adding, "Look, I'm only twenty-two, Dad. It's a five-year enlistment and I'll get out when I'm twenty-seven, still young enough to go into engineering."

I hoped that I was sounding sensible and responsible although neither of these had anything to do with my motivation. Honestly, I wasn't interested in a military career. The lure for me at the time was a glamorous lifestyle. Aware that it was probably selfish and could be hurtful to the family, I kept this kind of thinking to myself. I would just have to live with the fact that the celebration of my graduation on June 6, 1960, was a lot lower keyed than it might have been if I had been en route to hanging my diploma on the wall of a corporate office. MaMona, Uncle Al and Aunt Cecelia Sanchez and cousins Al and Linda came up from Salinas for the occasion. Whatever I planned to do, whatever I would do, I was the first person in the Alvarez/Sanchez clans to earn a college degree, and I think all of us at that gathering sensed we were at the beginning of a breakthrough for a new generation.

ORDERS CAME TO REPORT to the navy installation at the Oakland Airport at 7:30 A.M. on June 23, 1960, bringing only a small bag with a change of underwear. My father drove me up, dropped me at the gate, shook hands and said, "Good luck, son." It was as much emotion as he could show; he had never shaken my hand before. But my thoughts were all on the big adventure ahead, and the state of my nerves turned the next hour into what could have been a beginning for one of those TV military sitcoms.

I was scheduled out on a series of commercial flights to Pensacola, Florida, by way of Texas. The comedy began when the yeoman at the recruiting office gave me a slip of paper and said, "To save time why don't you take this yourself to the disbursement office for a TR—downstairs, out of the hangar, turn left, down a block." I ran all the way, arriving panting and asked an old chief petty officer, "Is this the dispensary?" He gave me an odd look and said, "No, it's thataway about six blocks." I at least sensed something was wrong and it must have shown on my face. "What are you looking for?" the chief asked. "A TR, whatever that is." He laughed. "A travel request, and you get it right here." I had to go on being dumb. "What's a dispensary?" He really roared. "That's a hospital, fella, this here's disbursement."

That was not the end. The commander assigned to swearing me in was late, and the yeoman had to drive me at full speed to the commercial terminal at the other end of the airport to catch my plane. At the gate I saw a DC-6 with hatch open and engines turning. A stewardess stood inside the open hatch. I asked a purser if I could make the flight. "If you try," he said. I waved at the stewardess, she waved back. I jumped over the gate and ran for the plane. I saw the stewardess apparently saying something to the pilots. The engines stopped. I tossed my little bag through the hatch, jumped high enough to get a grip on the sill and wriggled onto the floor of the plane. Looking down on me, the stewardess said, "If you had waited a couple of minutes we would have put the steps down for you." A minute later the purser arrived with steps and other passengers began to board. The plane was just landing, not taking off.

With a start like that, there was nowhere to go but up in my naval career, and it did take a turn for the better on the flight from Texas to Florida when I met two fellow cadets, Bob Phillips from North Texas State and Bob Crippen, an aeronautical engineer from the University of Texas. We arrived in Pensacola on a Friday afternoon and didn't have to report at the base until midnight Saturday. We decided to pool our resources and rent a hotel room with an extra cot for the night so that we could do some sightseeing the next day. I lost the toss and had to sleep on the cot.

We took a bus to the base in late afternoon. There was a walk of nearly a mile under a hot Florida sun to what they called the Indoctrination Battalion. Phillips and I had only our small bags, as instructed, but Crippen was lugging a suitcase like it was full of lead bricks. Tall and skinny, he was bent under the burden. "What the hell's in there, Crippen?" I asked.

"My aeronautical textbooks," he said.

Well, right away I figured I had run into a kindred soul. (I couldn't know then, of course, that I had just met the man who would command the space shuttle *Columbia* on its maiden voyage twenty-one years later.)

Reaching our destination in a sweat, we stood in awe of a beautiful, white-columned three-story brick building in Southern Colonial style. Almost reverently we mounted a circular staircase with marble steps. (This posh establishment, we soon learned, would be our quarters for only the first of sixteen weeks of preflight training.) We were dispatched to a barracks with the descriptive name of "Splinterville." But neither elegance nor comfort was a major consideration during that intense time of study, parade drill, weapons instruction, physical training. We were under the sharp eye and sharper tongue of a classically ill-tempered drill sergeant. On our first night in Splinterville my three roommates and I flunked room inspection. One of them who had come up through the ranks said, "I'm not going to take this kind of crap any more," and walked out of our lives forever.

I wasn't too crazy about that aspect of training either. I ranked about third in the class in academics and did well in physical training, which I enjoyed—with the possible exception of jumping into the pool from a thirty-foot tower without breaking anything. But in the third category we were graded on—officerlike qualities that comprised the way we drilled, dressed and generally comported ourselves—I nearly got tossed out. Using a roommate's clippers, I tried to augment my bimonthly $34 pay by undercutting (literally) the base barber and giving haircuts for twenty-five cents. Since this activity was illegal, I was careful to collect all the hair in a bag that I hid in an empty room. One day the drill sergeant found the bag, identified the culprit and dressed me down in unprintable language as lacking those necessary "officerlike qualities."

Nevertheless, I was made a class cadet officer and battalion subcommander, the last with the right to wear two bars. After commissioning I was sent off to Saufley Field on the other side of Pensacola for preliminary flight training. It wasn't exactly like being discharged from the Hanoi Hilton, but at that time in my life the feeling of hard-won freedom was a heady one. No longer would we have to march everywhere, and our off duty time was our own. Moreover, I was rich—base pay of $212 a month plus $100 flight pay plus $48 subsistence.

I WAS VERY COMFORTABLE in the cockpit; not so my roommate. Just before Christmas break he told me that he'd asked for a transfer to maintenance school. "Ev, this isn't for me," he said. "Every time I was up there I was scared." It seemed a shame after surviving preflight training. They say that sometimes fear is contagious, but fortunately it wasn't so with me. The next stage in training would be either in propeller planes, including helicopters, or in jets. I requested jets. Unfortunately a hundred other trainees were hoping for jets, too, and there were only about ten openings. I eased the tension of waiting out a decision by getting two other cadets from California to join me in driving my 1960 Chevy home for the holidays. It was a good family time with an all-is-forgiven air to it. Everybody wanted to pose for pictures with me in my dress blues, and Dad and Delia wanted to drive my car. I was starting to date Tangee, who, of course, would become my wife.

I headed back to Florida full of high hopes, but at Saufley I picked up the bad news—still no jets. My orders were to T-28's at Whiting Field in Milton, Florida, about forty miles away. Still, I knew that there would be another chance for jets at the end of basic training and decided the way to get there was to fly as well as I possibly could. Apparently the same kind of coordination that served me in athletics helped in flying. I felt in tune with the plane. When the instructor of another cadet took me up he said, "I wish so-and-so could fly like you. He has a death grip on the stick, you're smooth." The other cadet did wash out, as it happened, and I began to luck out.

With consistent good weather I was able to finish my syllabus at Whiting ahead of the pack and go back to Saufley for carrier qualification in the T-28. This consisted of landing over and over again in a space the size of a carrier's deck marked out on the field until judgment became instinct. It took a month, but on Memorial Day, 1961, I flew out to sea with a small group of fellow cadets to land on a ship. It was a glorious May day. As I circled in the sunny sky watching the others go down to land, I thought that I had never seen a sight more beautiful than the sleek gray hull of the carrier parting the blue sea into a sparkling white wake. This was what Navy flying was all about! I was very confident. I had mastered the pinpoint landing through coordinated control. I had mastered this thing, and now I was actually doing it. I pictured myself as one of the World War II pilots I had seen in old movies. Down I went and landed, if I do say so, like a gull. I was still in the running for jets.

The Navy must think that suspense is good for the soul. My orders to Advanced Training Command at Corpus Christi, Texas, didn't specify whether I would get into jets or be shunted off into multiengine craft. Cruising west in the Chevy Impala was an anxious time, but when I reported in on a Monday morning in June, I was elated to find orders to Kingsville for jet training in the F-9-F and ultimately the supersonic F-11-F. The only part of that training that gave me any trouble was flying in close formation at such high speeds, but I finally got the feel of that.

What I recall most vividly from that period was a lesson that had nothing to do with technical skill. Just the opposite. My instructor was a Marine captain with a liking for nicknames. One day when I complained of not seeing well he picked up on it and called me "Cousin Weakeyes." The captain and two other instructors decided to take three of us in separate planes on a weekend training flight to Dallas, possibly because the instructors' wives were living there. When they left us to fend for ourselves over Saturday night at the BOQ (bachelor officers' quarters), one cadet remembered that he had a cousin who was a Braniff stewardess. Luckily she was home and rounded up two other Braniff girls for a night on the town. We didn't get back to BOQ until 5:30 A.M. Sunday and were still standing under cold showers in an effort to clear our heads when our instructors arrived for the flight back to Kingsville. My Marine captain decided that it was the perfect time to practice instrument flying. He made me take off under the hood and keep it closed the whole way although it was boiling hot. I was sweating, my stomach was knotted with tension because the captain kept failing my instruments from his control panel to see how I would react. Somehow I managed to land blind at Kingsville, climbed out of the cockpit and started throwing up. While I was retching the captain said in a sweetly reasonable tone, "What's the matter, Cousin Weakeyes? Aren't you feeling well? Let this be a lesson to you. We pilots can go have a good time but when the time comes to fly that plane we have to fly it." It was an unforgettable lesson.

WINGS WERE PINNED on me at a low-keyed ceremony in the captain's office in Kingsville on November 14, 1961, but my feelings on that day were anything but low-keyed. I was truly up and away! My level of confidence had reached a new high. I had done it—done it well. That went for the survival courses they put us through as well as the flying. In the first survival course at the end of preflight training they had dropped us in the Florida woods for three days without food or equipment but a hunting knife. We dined on roots and pine-needle soup and even roasted a black snake that was as tough as it was tasteless. We learned something about hunger then and what it can do to human beings when the instructor tossed a can of K-rations into a busload of us heading back to base and laughed while the potential officers and gentlemen fought like animals over it. The second course was on the beaches and in the boondocks outside of San Diego, where we were "captured" and treated as the POWs in Korea had been. The instructors were very intimidating. So were some of their neat little tricks like stuffing us in tiny boxes for half an hour or so. I made it through both of these, as did most of my fellow trainees, with the sublime optimism—and ignorance—of youth: "This will never happen to me. . . ."

SINCE TANGEE AND I were getting serious about each other I asked for assignment to Lemoore Naval Air Station, within striking distance of her home in San Jose. I was put into a replacement air group and checked out on the A-4 Skyhawk to be ready to go into one of the fleet squadrons. A single engine, semidelta wing craft, the Skyhawk was designed in the late sixties for air-to-ground work and, specifically, as a carrier plane that could deliver the atomic weapon of the time—a big, big bomb. It had two 20 mm. machine guns and could carry rockets and other bombs under the wings. As a man with wings, I was flying high figuratively as well as literally. Six of us bachelors at Lemoore rented a cottage at Bass Lake, two hours away in the foothills of the Sierras. On Friday afternoons we would load our cars with beer and water-skiing equipment and dates and head off for a week-end. Now married and in college working toward an architectural degree, the same cousin Al who had considered me too sober in Santa Clara thought that I had had a complete personality implant.

I was reflecting the camaraderie and humor of my fellow fighter pilots. High jinks and self-deprecating, down-playing patter were the way we handled the tensions of a high-risk job and the close quarters aboard ship. This kind of behavior was virtually new to me. Living at home so much of the time, I had had very little experience of mingling with peers in college or academy.

On my first cruise aboard *Constellation*, a bunch of us in squadron 144 were sitting around having a beer at an officers' club in Okinawa, and the squadron leader pointed out a bar stool decked out in international orange, the squadron colors. "Wouldn't that look good in our ready room?" he said. Leaving the question dangling in air, he took off. Three of us wrapped the stool in a table cloth, walked it out of the club and through the woods to the pier. The carrier's captain was just pulling away in his launch, and he offered us a ride. One of us came up with an excuse for declining, but when we approached the ship on another tender we still had to get by the officer of the deck with something that looked like a mummy in white shrouds. Luckily we faced a very junior officer, and Nick Nicholson, a man with an air of command, ran interference for us. "I just want you to close your eyes, son," he said. "We're bringing something aboard." The stool graced our ready room until we suffered a form of just retribution: somebody else on the ship stole it from us.

Our brand of humor is more difficult to recapture than the high jinks. It tended to be spontaneous, spur of the moment, situational. I can't recall any instances from the early days but a few from the time of captivity are unforgettable. One occurred as we were being driven back to camp in a truck after that march through the streets of Hanoi when we had all been terrified by angry crowds that cursed, shoved, stoned and spat at us. Shot down a few months earlier, Jerry Coffee had been brought to Hanoi only the day before. As we bumped gloomily along nursing our hurts, Jerry asked, "Hey, fellows, does this happen every Saturday night in Hanoi?" One of Bob Shumaker's favorites credits me with the punch line. He and Smitty Harris shared a cell next door to Tom Barrett and me, and we communicated by tapping on the walls. So that Smitty could learn to play the piano, he and Bob had laboriously constructed a piano keyboard by drawing it on toilet paper with little sticks burned into charcoal. One morning Smitty tapped: "How are you all?" Tom tapped back: "Alvie's sort of down; must be that time of the month." Smitty replied: "Tell him I'll play a little music to cheer him up." After hours of silence, Smitty asked: "Well, how did Alvie like the music?" This time I took over. "Pretty good for ragtime," I tapped. Another POW, Scotty Morgan, was responsible for lifting spirits of the whole camp. A guard nicknamed Rudolph, because of his red nose, asked Scotty to teach him English; Scotty obliged. All day long Rudolph would go from cell to cell, grinning and saying, "I am queer. I am queer." (You do what you can.)

IN THE NAVY I did learn, as Al detected, how to take things by lightening up—and none too soon. When really put to the test I realized that humor could be at least as important as courage; in fact, humor could be called a kind of courage, a very effective whistling in the dark. On top of the thrill of flying, the good humor and camaraderie no doubt had a lot to do with the fact that I truly enjoyed being a fighter pilot. And I wasn't all that eager to become an engineer even after I took on the responsibility of marrying Tangee. My thoughts didn't project much beyond the next flight when I stood on *Constellation*'s deck and waved to Tangee and Delia, who were watching from the tip of Point Loma outside San Diego as I set off on what would be my last cruise.

As far as I was concerned, there wasn't anything like a real war going on out there in Southeast Asia to worry about, and I was leaving behind what looked like a happy family. A good girl of Mexican heritage, Tangee seemed to fit right into the scene at Santa Clara. Dad was holding onto a steady job and Mother was able to at last devote time and attention to Madeleine. Delia was doing well at San Jose State, the first girl in the extended family to get a college education. Still close to her, I had felt fortunate to be able not only to repay what she had loaned me but also to help her get out of the house and room with some other college girls, by sending her $35 a month to cover her share of the rent. The sum had amounted to $350, and just before boarding my ship I told her to forget it; it was no longer a loan but a gift. I was sailing away with sweet memories and a good conscience. And sublime ignorance of what waited for me, including eight and a half years of captivity.

CHAPTER VI

Learning to Cry Again

"IT IS VERY DIFFICULT to describe the nothingness of those years in prison camp—the sheer boredom of the experience," I told a reporter who interviewed me shortly after Tammy and I arrived in Kingsville, Texas, in the fall of 1973. "We were stagnant, put in a Mason jar with the lid screwed on and put on a shelf. The hardest part of it was the nothing. After a while, it seemed like a dream."

Nowhere could those lost years have taken on a more dreamlike aspect than in Kingsville. I was picking up life where I had left off—in the air. I was flying again and loving every minute of it, because I was recapturing some of the insouciance and confidence of youth in the process. There were ten of us POWs in the program, and we shared that special fighter pilot camaraderie, reinforced by what we had been through together in Vietnam. Most of us had wives with us, and many of them, like Tammy, were pregnant. We were all getting a second chance at carving out careers and creating families. It was the future that enthralled us—although the past was always there.

The three months at Kingsville were a honeymoon. We enjoyed getting to know each other, and we both were excited

Wide-eyed about the prospects of a life together, Tammy and I posed in November, 1973, outside our first home, an apartment in Kingsville, Texas.

by the prospect of becoming parents at relatively advanced ages—she at thirty-four, I at thirty-six. For different reasons, we both looked forward to the move to Monterey. Much as I loved flying, I knew that sticking with it wouldn't be compatible with the close family relationship I craved. It would mean long tours of sea duty. I also wouldn't be equipped for another career if I reached a dead end. Since my course at the Naval Postgraduate School in Monterey would take two years, we could settle down and buy a house where Tammy

Before I could get back into a real cockpit, I had to be checked out in a trainer at Kingsville.

A ground school refresher was also part of the Kingsville program.

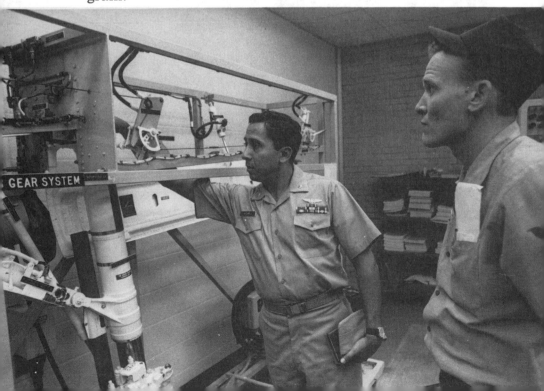

GEAR SYSTEM

could exercise her homemaking talents to the fullest in a more interesting community.

After the first flurry of interviews at Kingsville, I fell out of sight as far as the celebrity circuit was concerned. But when Christmas rolled around it became apparent that I hadn't fallen out of some influential minds. One of these belonged to a Texan, the entrepreneur H. Ross Perot, who wrote to me:

Christmas and freedom have a special meaning to you.
You and your freedom have a special meaning to all of us.
—You never gave up.
—The American people never forgot you.
—We will never forget you and the other brave men who fought and died for us.
Each Christmas while you were away, millions of Americans prayed for your safe return. Throughout the years they worked—mobilizing world opinion to improve your treatment. Never before had so many expressed so much concern for so few.
On your first Christmas back home, we celebrate with you, and thank you for all you have done for your country. Keep your high ideals and patriotism untarnished over the years. May the future bring you added happiness and joy to offset the years you gave up for us.
God bless you.

The other person who kept us in mind was a Californian—Governor Ronald Reagan—whose Christmas letter was a form of welcome back to my home state:

Dear Tammy and Everett:

You certainly have brightened our Christmas with your letter and card, particularly the expression of your happiness in this first Christmas at home in ten years.
You might as well reconcile yourself with that other news you wrote—your child already has an Aunt Nancy. We are both delighted that you are going to be back in California.
I try to think of just what this Christmas must have meant to you and I don't suppose, with utmost imagination, I can

even come close. I do know this, though, we have you to thank for a great many Christmases for the rest of us. You and all those who shared your experiences.

Nancy and I will look forward to seeing you both, in fact, all three of you, here in California in the days ahead.

Bless you both, and have a wonderful new year.

Another California welcome came from our friend Jim Shea who loaned us his town house on the bay at Monterey while we were making arrangements for our own place. Bob Shumaker was already going to school there when we arrived, and he put us in touch with a real estate agent, an ex-Navy type, who evidently thought that POWs developed common tastes in captivity. He may have been right. We ended up

The former POWs retraining at Kingsville pose at a "Wetting Down Party" at the base officers' club. Among them are members of our wedding party—Dave Carey, best man, in the center next to me in a light sport coat; Chuck Rice and Charlie Zuhoski, third and second from the right. (*Official U.S. Navy Photo*)

For Tammy and me, Kingsville was a honeymoon, but it was hard finding time alone like this with all the friendly POWs around.

buying a house that Bob had nearly purchased. It was a three bedroom, split-level ranch house on Greenwood Way off Skyline Drive. Nestled in woods, it was visited by deer and raccoons and would have had a magnificent view of Monterey and the bay below except for the trees.

Just before we moved to Monterey, I got the news that the family housing at Lemoore Naval Air Station had been named "Alvarez Village." What I liked most about this compliment was that the name hadn't been decreed by the brass or picked out of a hat. It had been decided in a contest with an award of a $25 U.S. Savings Bond going to each of two winners—a civilian employee on the base and the wife of an enlisted man. But I wasn't the only member of the family to be honored at that time. Even though she had left her job in October, Tammy was named eastern division special achievement award winner for 1973 by United Airlines. At the banquet ceremony in Washington's Mayflower Hotel, I was able to sit back and applaud *her* for a change.

Tammy really deserved a bigger and better award for putting up with me. I was still hiding behind that Plexiglas emotional screen that I had brought all the way from Hanoi. When she asked, I would disclose bits and pieces of my Vietnam experience, but she did have to ask. I seldom volunteered anything. I can still hear her saying, "You can tell me,

Everett, I'm your *wife.*" She tried to establish communications between me and my family, too. Coming from a talkative family, she was exasperated by our tight-lipped behavior. My mother would sometimes wonder aloud about what I had done or was thinking, and Tammy would say, "Why don't you ask *him*? He's your *son*." Tammy was particularly upset when I wouldn't, as she put it, "live out an argument." Rather than fight over some emotional issue—usually the way my family was reacting to our marriage—I would keep silent or walk away.

This was not really conscious behavior on my part. I was obeying the instinct for self-preservation that had surfaced in captivity. I had been forced to live alone for six months without knowing that there was another American anywhere in North Vietnam and for months after that with only sporadic, minimal and dangerous communication with men in other cells. Having only my own thoughts as company, I quickly discovered that worry about what my loved ones far away were doing and thinking was self-destructive. For as long as I remained in prison, their well-being and happiness would remain beyond my control. Letting myself stew about them would only result in a cancer of frustration. Even when I began to have cellmates I had to keep myself aloof enough to be able to tolerate it when they were taken off at a whim. All this may not be an adequate excuse, but it is an explanation for the way I was. The best I can come up with.

Tammy, bless her, was for the most part understanding. She is a people person. Psychology was her minor in college, and her professional life was devoted to pleasing people of all kinds. But there was one occasion not long after we settled into our house in Monterey when her understanding wore thin.

My father had just dropped in for a rare visit. Tammy had just returned from a two-week stay in Pittsburgh where she had been helping her mother get through her grandmother's death. I was finding conversation with Dad rather sticky since he and Mother were in the process of divorce. Then the phone rang. It was Tammy's brother-in-law with the bad news that her father had suffered a heart attack. Tammy retreated to the bedroom to talk to him and came out crying. Apparently they didn't think the attack was bad enough for her to return to Pittsburgh, but my reaction to a crisis like that was to do something. Knowing how close she was to her father, I asked her, "Do you want to get on a plane and go back home, honey?" Still crying, she shook her head. I shrugged and turned back to deal with my father. "Can I get you a beer, Dad?" I asked. I heard Tammy gasp, heard the bedroom door slam. My head told me that she wanted me to show more distress, to weep with her, but I just couldn't do it—not then. Not yet.

AT THAT TIME I couldn't get my act together in public either. I was being asked to speak here and there and would go if I couldn't get out of it gracefully. But I didn't know what my message ought to be. I didn't know what people wanted to hear, what they were willing to hear. I wasn't far enough away from the experience to see the woods for the trees, and I was still conscious of my deficiencies as an orator. The closest I came to distilling some pure stream of thought out of that swamp of miserable events in Vietnam was a paper I wrote for my course in behavioral science. It was about how we had utilized the sense of sound in prison. As the title of the paper's first section—"The Nothingness of Four Walls"—would indicate, I was stressing the theme of deprivation just as I had in my interview at Kingsville.

Reviewing that paper today, I realize that I was also beginning to get a handle on the positive side of the experience. I began by describing the typical cell—seven feet by seven feet, blank concrete walls and concrete floor, small ventilation ducts near the fifteen-foot ceiling, two concrete slabs as beds, heavy steel reinforced door that might have a pinhole bored through by a termite. Belongings for each inmate consisted of a straw mat, a mosquito net, a water jug, a metal cup, one blanket, a set of prison pajamas, two pairs of shorts—and a "Bo," a small bucket that served as commode, sink, stool.

Nothing whatever was provided for a prisoner to occupy his time. Some of us lived alone in such cells for up to two or three years.

"For almost all of our waking moments, there was nothing to see," I wrote. "One could just as well have closed his eyes, and kept them closed. (Some, for the most part, did just that.) There was very little to touch or feel. And most of us who spent a very long period of time in solitary confinement may just as well have lost the ability to talk. We had no one to talk to.

"Out of necessity, we had to adapt ourselves to a new manner of living. We depended primarily on sound. We came to know our new immediate world through its sounds. From the time the gongs would ring in the early morning until they rang again at night, marking the end of another day, familiar noises filled the long hours signifying the passing events of the daily routines.

"We learned to tell by the particular way the turnkey rattled his key ring who the guard was for that day. We could tell by the way he handled his keys and the rate at which he opened the cell doors if anything unusual was happening or if he was in a good or sour mood.

"We could tell by the particular creaking noises the doors made as they were being swung open whose cell it was. The shuffling noises as the rubber sandals scraped along the concrete floors gave us the clue as to who was out of his cell washing himself or dumping his 'Bo.' We learned to recognize each prisoner's particular cough, or the way he cleared his throat, or wheezed, or sniffled.

"We also learned to keep an open ear for danger signs—especially when we were engaged in some covert activity, such as communicating. The swishing of a guard's ammo belt against his trousers, or the pat of his gun butt against his leg, was a warning sound of a guard approaching. As we quietly pressed our ear against a crack in the door or lay on the floor with our ear against a rat hole at the bottom of the door, these same noises indicated if the guard was equipped with an AK-45 semiautomatic rifle or an old World War II model carbine. We could even tell by the combinations of many

I don't look as uncomfortable as I felt when somebody snapped this picture of me delivering one of my first speeches—to a Navy League dinner while I was a student at Monterey. Not only am I shy by nature, but in those days I didn't know what my message about my experience ought
to be.

noises that he generated where he was looking and at what he was looking. Unbeknownst to the guards, they were under constant sensory observation the entire time they were in the area of the cell blocks."

I explained that the kind of sensory deprivation that we suffered caused depression, loss of appetite, nightmares, hallucinations. We realized that we had to fight against these disorders, and our only weapon was sound. With sound, we could communicate with each other. At great risk we did, saving our sanity and maybe our lives. This communication took some ingenuity!

"We soon discovered the brick walls to be excellent conductors of sound. A light tap with the fingernail could be clearly heard if the man on the opposite side of the wall pressed his ear to the wall. And there was no danger of the noise being heard outside the cell block by a roving guard. Soon a completely new alphabet was devised utilizing the tapping sound (similar to Morse code). The use of it extended to where message traffic was flowing continually from one end of a cell block to another; then, later, from cell block to cell block, from building to building.

"In a couple of maximum security type camps, the cells were separated by double walls; i.e., a void space between the two walls so as to cut out communication by tapping. The guards were doubled as a protection against any known noise communications. In these camps, the means of sending code developed through the use of 'natural' and sometimes guttural noises a person made, such as a cough, a clearing of the throat, a sneeze, a belch, a burp, a blowing of the nose. Each of these sounds, or a combination of some, represented a letter of the alphabet under this system. It was found that through the silent, echoing passageways of the cell block, these noises were conducted quite easily. I heard of one individual living in one of these camps who would pretend sleep for a couple of hours each day during the siesta hours, and through his snoring managed to send complete messages, telling how everyone was and what was going on in his cell block.

"The transition from the normal way of life to one of deprivation was difficult indeed. To recognize the routes which one could take to be able to cope with the situation was challenging. And what *was* a wonderment of surprise to most of us was the way we could exist in this new way of life; the countless joys we received from some exchanges that were transmitted through the walls, the sorrow we all felt to hear some depressing news that came from a message sent from somewhere beyond the walls, and the numerous times our spirits were bolstered by a few well-coined phrases tapped out by a friend who somehow knew how we felt at the time."

My professor's notes on the paper—"Very good ... you write *very* well ... Sensitive analysis—Very perceptive, thoughtful"—gave me at least some hope that I could develop a message worth passing along. Meanwhile, I had my hands full getting back into the swing of a tough academic program. I was studying operations research and systems analysis, a curriculum that would lead to a master of science degree.

I didn't know exactly where I was going or what I would do with this education but I felt that I was on my way and wasn't about to let anything stop me. Neither was Tammy. When we would fend off invitations or cut short social engagements on the grounds of my need to work, we apparently hurt some people. Since Tammy was usually the one who had to do this, she was seen as driving a wedge between me and the family. In spite of what Cousin Al, for one, knew about me from Santa Clara days, they couldn't believe that I was that involved, and they thought that Tammy was either overprotecting me or using me as an excuse to avoid contact. If we were indulging in self-protection it wasn't for me alone. Tammy was wholly absorbed in the impending arrival of a baby. She was having a difficult time carrying it toward the end, and her doctor wanted her to stay in bed as much as possible.

With indications that the baby might come early, the weeks of June, 1974, were an anxious, nervous time in the Alvarez household. The people who credit me with being calm in crisis should have seen me in those days. On June 19 we had a guest for dinner—a POW friend, Bill Metzger, who had come up from his station in San Diego to look into a possible curriculum at the school. Tammy said that she didn't feel like cooking so we all went down to Pacific Grove for a Chinese dinner, someone joking on the way that the Chinese food might loosen things up. Bill disappeared after dinner, and we went to bed because Tammy was very tired. In the middle of the night, she started getting regular pains. She called the doctor, who told her to get right over to the hospital.

Then we thought her water broke. I told her to stand in the shower while I ran around scooping a blanket off the bed. A little confused and frightened, Tammy obeyed me but asked from the shower stall, "Why are you getting a blanket?"

A good question in late June in California. "I don't know," I said. "Doesn't everybody get a blanket when taking a wife to the hospital?"

Then: "Why am I standing here?"

"So the floor won't get wet."

Tammy's saner head took over. "This is ridiculous," she said and got out of the shower.

Fortunately for our safety on the road with me at the wheel, the hospital was only two blocks away. Once we got there it appeared that we might be in for a long wait. I sat with Tammy in the labor room, holding her hand. There was a phone that the nurse said could be used to call out but nobody could call in. Shortly after we arrived I heard it ringing, picked it up and found my mother-in-law in Pittsburgh at the other end of the wire. She hadn't been able to be with Tammy because of her husband's heart attack, but being resourceful she had evidently used his medical contacts to reach us. During the day, Bill Metzger showed up to cheer us on and bring food. Finally, Tammy's doctor who had canceled a trip to be on hand for her delivery gave her medication to induce labor.

When the time came, the doctor let me scrub up with him and follow Tammy into the delivery room. I stood by her head, holding her hand and trying to help her with the breathing exercises she had been taught. And then the miracle came to pass. A wriggling red baby boy slid out into the doctor's waiting hands. They cleaned him, wrapped him in a blanket and handed him to me. While I held this feather-weight package the baby opened one eye and looked up at me as if to ask, "And who are you?" At that moment, I knew exactly who I was: I was his father, charged with loving and caring for him. His mouth opened, and he let out a lusty cry. What a feeling! What joy! I looked from the baby back to Tammy, exhausted but happy, and filled to overflowing with emotion. I was crying, flooding with uncontrollable tears for the first time since my unexpected encounter with Nick Nicholson in Hawaii.

The Plexiglas shield was melting down. I could *feel* and give way to my feelings almost as I had when I was young and trusting, in the days before I was told that men don't cry. This time, as I grew up again into the new life ahead of me as father and husband, I would let myself cry in both joy and sadness. I had nothing to prove in the way of manhood and much to gain in moments like this.

We had decided to name a boy Marc, and I said, "Hello, Marc. I'm your dad, and I'm glad you're here."

CHAPTER VII

Go East, Young Man

WHILE TAMMY AND I were preoccupied with our new son a tragedy was unfolding daily on TV. Richard Nixon was sinking deeper and deeper into the mire of Watergate. Crediting him with my freedom as I did, I suffered through those hearings. Once my sister Delia, who had loudly opposed Nixon and his policies, was watching with me and she surprised me by saying, "It's a good thing this didn't happen earlier, Everett, or you guys would still be in Hanoi." We hadn't yet sat down to talk over our political differences, but Delia's offhand remark indicated that we might be able to manage some degree of understanding.

The disruption in Washington was bound to lead to a deterioration of affairs in Vietnam. Once American forces were withdrawn and the nation's attention turned inward, it was inevitable that our South Vietnamese allies would be overwhelmed by the North Vietnamese, whose fierce determination I knew only too well. In the winter and early spring of '75 the North Vietnamese rolled south until we were finally treated to pictures in living color of Americans running for helicopters to lift them out of a falling Saigon. I was sad to see it, and I guess I should have been bitter, but I wasn't. It seemed to be in keeping with everything else going on—a negative image of Vietnam veterans, nobody wanting to talk about the war, everybody anxious to have it over with. I just thought: Well, so be it. Let's get on with our lives. Forget the past.

Easy to think; hard to do. The media came after us POWs— the unforgotten Vietnam vets—right away to see how we felt about the bitter end to the war. I was called by the CBS-TV station in Los Angeles. They wanted to come up the next day to interview and photograph me on "a typical morning." Although I told them that I didn't have much to say, they were insistent, persuasive. I didn't tell them that on "a typical morning" in the Alvarez household I slid out of bed, kissed a sleepy Tammy and a sleeping baby goodbye and headed for school. Getting up early to make breakfast wasn't Tammy's bag. She had tried it once soon after the wedding and we both agreed that it wasn't a good idea. But I suspected that things would be different when I told her that a TV crew was arriving, and I knew it for sure when she went right out to have her hair done.

When I woke up the next morning Tammy was nowhere to be seen. By the time I walked into the kitchen I was greeted by unbelievable sights, sounds, and smells. The TV people were already on the scene, setting up lights and cameras. All dolled up with a fancy apron, Tammy was presiding over a stove with a pan of sizzling bacon and eggs, a pot bubbling with coffee. Marc, scrubbed and dressed in a white shirt and bow tie, sat in his high chair watching her in open-mouthed astonishment. They wanted me to partake of this "typical" feast while I talked. So between bites and sips I told them that whatever the outcome, the cause in Vietnam was a good cause, and I felt we had a right to be there in defense of democracy.

They didn't listen long enough for me to finish breakfast. The reporter broke off, went to the kitchen phone and got his producer in Los Angeles on the line. Whether intentionally or not, he spoke loudly enough for me to hear: "Well, he says the same things as the rest of them. Got nothing new here." They were polite as they packed away their gear, but they were obviously disappointed. What do they want of us—a weepy confession that we suffered for nothing? I thought. Well, they'll never get it from me. The best news of the day was the reporter's admission that the other POWs were saying the same thing.

There was a postscript: At a POW gathering at San Clemente a year or so later this same reporter came up to me and said, "I'll bet you don't remember me, Commander Alvarez." I said, "I sure do. Your visit was the last time I had breakfast during the week before going to work."

WHEN DR. ILYAS WAS WELL enough to fly, Tammy's parents came out to visit us and see their new grandson. I admired the doctor for more than his accomplishments. He had seen a lot of life and acquired a lot of wisdom. He was a man of compassion. Just one illustration: When he was serving as a doctor at an Army base in the South, a maid kidnapped Tammy's sister, then an infant. Once the baby was returned Dr. Ilyas refused to prosecute on the grounds that the woman had been driven to her act by her circumstances. He was also a man of fierce patriotism, as naturalized citizens often are. He considered America the greatest land on earth because of the opportunities it had presented to him, and he would die whispering, "God bless America." Love for America and respect for its institutions were attitudes that my father-in-law and I deeply shared. When he spoke I listened, as during the sightseeing trips we took together around Monterey.

I showed him the posh resort turned academy where I studied, the famed seventeen-mile drive along the coast. When we paused at a lookout point he shook his head in wonderment at the scenery. "This is all very beautiful. But what are you studying? What is it that you are going to do with your life?"

Without much success I tried to explain systems analysis. I told him I had selected it from other options because it involved a great deal of math, which I liked. When he persisted—"And what can you do with that?"—I found that I really couldn't explain. "Well, it's good background for engineering or management or whatever," I said.

"Now, you are still a young man, Everett," he said. "Have you ever thought about law school or medical school?"

I confessed that I had—in my days of dreaming in prison. But when I got back, three years in law school or four years in medical school seemed an intolerable additional delay in getting on with my life. I thought I should stick to the technical, build on my engineering foundation. Dr. Ilyas's argument was that in the long run it was more practical to lay the groundwork for becoming independent. Although he never regretted serving his country as a military physician, there came a time when he felt that the regimentation and limits in military life prevented him from practicing the way he knew he should, from making the most of his talents. He foresaw that I might arrive at the same point and wanted me to be prepared for it. He was, it turned out, planting seeds in my mind, but it would be a while before they sprouted.

There was another development during my in-laws' visit that would shape my future. When they talked back and forth, I realized that my wife and mother-in-law were the only two people I've ever met who did not like Monterey, California. For Mrs. Ilyas and Tammy, Pittsburgh, even before it was cleaned up, was God's country. In their minds, physical beauty could not compete with the presence of generations of family. And for Tammy, who was used to more urban living, there was a scary wildness to our Monterey surroundings that kept her on edge. Our house was on a cul-de-sac in the midst of a pine forest frequently and spookily shrouded in fog. Tammy, who was pregnant again not long after Marc's birth, was often alone there with the baby while I was at school and was frightened by strange sounds and sights. Once when her mother was there a picture fell from the wall in a distant room and within minutes they had police searching the house for the source of the noise. As though it were a sort of haunted house.

I'll never forget the afternoon that I arrived home to find a police car and fire truck blocking the driveway. With Marc in her arms, Tammy was pacing back and forth in front of the house. I parked in the street, jumped out of the car and ran to her. "What's happened? Is there a fire?"

Clutching Marc close to her, she just looked at me. "You're going to be mad at me but don't be. . . ."

I went into the house, and there, in the family room, stood a couple of burly firemen and a policeman. One of them was holding a wastebasket in his hand. "What's going on here?" I demanded.

Silently, the man held the wastebasket out toward me. I looked in and saw a gecko—a salamander about three inches long—scrambling around the bottom. "I don't think your wife likes it here," the man said as I tried to decide whether to laugh or cry.

I knew that Tammy was deathly afraid of creepy-crawly things and I certainly couldn't get mad at her when she told me the whole story. She had been in the kitchen with the doors open so that she could see down the hallway and into the bedroom where Marc was sleeping. She saw this thing, a strange creature, crawling up the walls. She forced herself to run past it, scoop up Marc and get to the family room, where she phoned the wife of another POW. From Tammy's description the woman thought that it might be a scorpion and advised her to call the police. I tried to calm her, telling her that geckos had been among my most welcome visitors in Vietnam because they would keep down the mosquito population in the cell. After that I devoted a lot of time to gecko-proofing the house.

We had almost as much trouble with the human population in Monterey. It was there that we first ran into an attitude that persists to this day not only in Monterey but in most other communities when it comes to POWs. For a year and a half we never exchanged words with our neighbors across the street, and as newcomers we were shy about approaching them. When the ice was finally broken we learned that, in fact, they had been reluctant to intrude on our privacy after

From our apartment in Kingsville to this woodsy home in the hills above Monterey, California, was a big move for both of us. Tammy posed with our first son, Marc, whose birth a year earlier released me from the emotional screen I had constructed around me to survive in prison.

what I had been through and because of all the publicity I'd had. To put it bluntly—people figured that I had to have some sort of psychological damage. Whether from misguided consideration, as was the case with our neighbors whom we finally got to know well, or a distaste for dealing with a person who might be strange, people often held themselves aloof. Stay away. Over the years Tammy has become incensed with people who ask her, out of my hearing, "Is he all right? Does he have nightmares . . . ?" Tammy isn't alone in this. The wife of Dick Stratton, a fellow POW who has since become a professional social worker to help really traumatized vets, says that after eighteen years people still pull her aside and whisper conspiratorially, "How *is* he, my dear?"

Considering all this, it was easier to do most of our infrequent socializing with the POWs who were resident in the Monterey area or who kept popping in and out. Gradually, though, we had to admit to ourselves that these gatherings were sort of boring. They usually involved swapping yarns about flying or prison days, since that was what we had in common, and drinking too much. I guess I was more interested in plans for the future than in going over the old ground again and again. I noticed that some others with ambitious programs, like Bob Shumaker or John McCain or Jerry Denton, were pulling away from the POW scene, and I was coming to the conclusion that I should do it, too, when a rather ugly happening made it necessary.

For reasons that made sense to us Tammy would take Marc with her and go to Pittsburgh for a week or two at a time. She was concerned about her father's frail health. Her trips were no strain on our finances because of her United passes, and my seven days—and sometimes nights—a week study schedule kept me busy while she was gone. We were perplexed when the POWs and their wives began acting cool toward Tammy; at one party, in fact, nobody would sit next to her. Finally Bill Metzger took it on himself to enlighten me and invited me out for a beer. "The wives are buzzing. The story's all around that you and Tammy are getting a divorce because she leaves you so much. . . ."

It seemed the POWs felt sorry for me and saw Tammy as the villain of the piece. I suppose they meant well, but it was hurtful. Bill was right about the rumors getting around the circuit. Tom Browning and his wife took the trouble to fly up for a visit with Tammy and me when they heard them. As he was leaving he told us, "I don't know what they're talking about, you guys are doing all right." After that Charlie

Zuhoski and Dave Carey began spreading the word in their own fashion: "What they're saying about Ev and Tammy is bullshit." The rumors stopped, but damage had been done.

INTEREST IN WHAT our nonexistence had done to us POWs physically and psychologically wasn't limited to family, friends, or neighbors. Almost immediately, the Navy launched a program unique for the military that still continues to study us scientifically. Navy and Marine POWs were given an opportunity to report voluntarily to the Naval Aerospace Medical Institute in Pensacola, Florida, for exhaustive annual examinations. More than a hundred of us took advantage of this, which has become a reunion with a purpose. With me, they discovered that I was host to microscopic parasites that can be eliminated with medication but return every so often. Like most of my fellow POWs, I also had lasting neurological-orthopedic damage—in my case from being bound. I've had weakness and tingling in the hands and fingers that has been relieved to an extent by operations to remove scar tissue from the ulnar nerve in the arm. To the surprise—and, I sometimes think, perhaps disappointment—of a lot of people, no serious psychological problems have so far been uncovered in me or some ninety-eight percent of the others during the annual testing.

I had thought—at least hoped—that I would soon be forgotten by the general public when I buried myself in the academic world at Monterey. Not so. Unexpected honors kept coming and reminding me of my at least symbolic status. In January, 1975, I was asked to speak in El Paso, Texas, at the dedication of a 100-unit low-income housing project named for me by the city's Housing Authority. Because it had no relationship to the military, I felt it was an honor of special significance for me, and it gave me a wonderful opportunity to say what I truly felt about all these occasions where I'd been singled out.

"I feel that this honor is a tribute not just to me but to all men who served in Southeast Asia—those who served,

In a small, quiet ceremony on January 15, 1975, at the Naval
Postgraduate School in Monterey, the awards for my service in
Vietnam were presented by the school's superintendent, Rear
Admiral Isham Linder. (*Official U.S. Navy Photo*)

suffered and gave their lives. It was faith that kept us going in
the prison cells of North Vietnam. What we see here today is a
fulfillment of that faith."

By then, I was also beginning to see the inequality between
the treatment given us POWs and the veterans returning
from the battlefields of South Vietnam. The only thing I could
do about it was to use my visibility to remind people of what
they had done. The honors that started coming through military channels at about the same time were a different matter.
I did accept them—a Silver Star, two awards of the Legion of
Merit and two awards of the Bronze Star. I'd served, I'd
earned them.

Our second truly blessed event at Monterey was the birth

Tammy began what has become a family tradition of involving the children in my public life by bringing six-month-old Marc to the decoration ceremonies in Monterey, where we posed for the Navy photographer. (*Official U.S. Navy Photo*)

on July 6, 1976, of another son, Bryan. Interesting omens surrounded this event. This high point in my life was the tenth anniversary of one of its lowest points—the humiliating and brutalizing prisoner march through the streets of Hanoi. At this time, too, the nation was celebrating the 200th anniversary of the Declaration of Independence. For me, though, Bryan's birth meant that I had a larger family to care for and an urgent need to make some career decision as my course of study wound down.

I knew, of course, that I would be staying in the Navy for a while. I had at least four years left to go before I would be eligible to retire with any pension benefits, but there were a variety of options about where and how I could spend those

I'm on the far right of the middle row of this 1976 graduating class in Operation Research and Systems Analysis at the Naval Postgraduate School. It was serious business—round-the-clock study for all of us—and we were obviously proud of ourselves for making the grade.

years. We POWs were still being given more or less carte blanche on assignments. I had already opted out of following the path toward promotion as a line officer, and the sensible thing for me to do was to find some area of shore duty where my graduate studies would prove useful. Much as I dreaded what I'd heard about its bureaucratic frustrations, Washington was where the action was to be found. It was also the place, next to Pittsburgh, that was closest to Tammy's heart and where she would be near her sister and old friends. We moved to Washington and I took a manager's course at the Fort Belvoir Defense Systems Management College while I waited for an active-duty post.

Unfortunately, relations with my immediate and extended family in California had not improved during our stay there. Along with the kind of misunderstanding we had had with my Sanchez cousins—they saw as my unwillingness what I saw as my inability as a Navy officer to get involved in the Chicano movement—we never did get around to any kind of open, meaningful discussion about our respective actions and feelings during the years of enforced separation. Now I was leaving again. It would have been harder to do if it hadn't been for my mother's amazing show of strength. A woman who had never gone anywhere without my father to take her, she had got her driver's license, gone to night school to complete a high school education, and was heading for a certificate in Early Childhood Programs from West Valley Joint Community College in Los Gatos so that she could work with young Hispanic children who were slow learners. No longer was Mother learning, or living, through her children.

While we were in Monterey, Mother would come up about once a month to visit us and her grandchildren. She and Tammy were never quite comfortable together, and she was acutely aware of all the other tensions in the family. During one visit she told Tammy, "If you stay here your marriage won't last." It was her way of saying go, of letting go—a form of a blessing on our decision to move east. I think we all knew, though, that my roots were too deep in California for this move to be any kind of a permanent separation.

CHAPTER VIII

The White House Is Calling

"TODAY HE CAN look out from his tenth floor office, across a park, and see the White House. In North Vietnam he couldn't see much of anything—especially his future," an interviewer for *Purple Heart* magazine wrote about me when I was appointed deputy administrator of the Veterans Administration. Perceptive and true. In the process of getting on with my life after those years in prison I saw, as you've seen, no fixed goal ahead of me. After all, I'd learned the hard way how unpredictable life can be. In the school of survival you're taught to adapt to circumstances, to practice the art of the possible, not hang onto unrealistic hopes and aspirations. With a master's degree from the Naval Post Graduate School in Monterey in my briefcase, I came to Washington in 1976 in search of good options rather than any specific employment, let alone "destiny."

If I hadn't already dropped the option of a lifetime naval career I would have soon come to that conclusion. Ironically, in spite of having an Annapolis graduate in the White House, the four years I had to serve out before retirement were discouraging for the military. President Jimmy Carter's granting of amnesty to young men who fled the country to escape service in Vietnam was, frankly, hard to take. I can concede now that amnesty may have helped the healing process, but at the time it seemed like a slap in the face, a devaluation of our service. Wrongly, in my view, much of the American public blamed the military for what had happened in Vietnam, with a consequent loss of pride and prestige for most anyone in uniform. In this atmosphere the possibility of a reduction in forces and loss of opportunity for advancement was always present.

I won't go into great detail about the period between coming to Washington and my first major government position —one, incidentally, that I would never have imagined for myself. After all, plenty of people discharged from service have gone through rigors, including disappointments, starts and stops and changes of direction.

Through it all I kept family my first priority and I'm glad I did. Partly it was due to my own family background, my lack of doing much with my father. Mostly, that was because there wasn't enough money, but the rare times he was able to take me places are still brightly etched in my memory. Okay, I'd do better—how many parents have said that?—with my boys. I can't say, though, that I've been as successful as I'd have liked to be, but excerpts from letters my sons wrote during these years at least show that maybe I didn't do too bad a job. "My father always works hard for our needs and always has time for us. He takes me to McDonalds on Saturday mornings for breakfast and talk," Marc wrote. And Bryan: "My dad always has time for us. My dad even skips business trips for us."

Well, I tried and I'm glad they felt that way, but the truth was that I felt I was away too much, that I needed a career, if possible, that would give some continuity and security for my family beyond the catch-as-catch-can of the jobs I'd had. I remembered my father-in-law's talk about being a lawyer, for example, and thought why not? Much of my work involved negotiating procurement contracts between government and private industry and handling disputes between them. Tammy was enthusiastic and not put off a minute by the several years it would take to get a law degree through night school, but some of our friends thought differently. They said I'd been through so much stress and strain that this could be just too much. I think they were showing, along with real concern, their feeling that I would break down. There was also an implication here that somehow Tammy was being too ambitious and driving me beyond my limits, and so forth. The truth was the opposite: she was letting me drive myself, freeing me up to fly as high as I could.

I couldn't wait to take off, never considering a crash landing. Georgetown University was my first stop, and I didn't linger when I found out I had to take the Legal Scholastic Aptitude Test and that the whole admissions process "can take a while," as the admissions office said. I'd been a year in Washington, was not innocent of red tape but not too tolerant of it either. And time was something that I didn't have to burn. I went for some advice to Ray Berg, who had been air intelligence officer aboard the *Constellation* when I was shot down and was now an attorney in Washington. He sent me to the dean of admissions of his alma mater, George Washington Law School, where things went much smoother and I entered the law school in the summer of 1978—I'd also been admitted to Georgetown, as it turned out.

What followed was a hectic schedule of study and Navy business. Here's Tammy's version of that time: "People would say you have to stop pushing him. I thought, if he wants it, let him go for it. They didn't know that Everett has a bottomless pit for absorbing knowledge. He loved it. It was hard in a way, but not really, because when you see your mate happier it makes life easier. We weren't Ozzie and Harriet, but it was worth it."

She was right, I did love it, and it wasn't easy for any of us. During this time nobody much pressed for interviews or speaking engagements, which was good. But there was one appearance in July of 1979 that I especially enjoyed. It was at the Lemoore Naval Air Station's observance of national POW-MIA Recognition Day, and I got a chance to fly across country in an A-7. It was a homecoming of sorts. My name was on the housing at Lemoore, and the man who came to meet me was my old friend Nick Nicholson, now a retired Navy Captain of the carrier *Ranger*. He took me to the officers' club, where I was surrounded by young men who were truly interested in my experiences as a POW. There were other POWs on the program, too, and for the first time I felt comfortable in talking about the imprisonment and its aftermath. Where possible, I tried to be sort of light about it. I was grateful that the papers picked up a message that I wanted to get across to the public on behalf of other POWs as well as myself:

"People come up to me and say, 'You look well. Are you normal?'" I told the audience. "My answer is always, 'I don't know. What's normal?' People ask my wife, 'Does he sleep well? Does he have nightmares?' She always says, 'He sleeps like a log—and talk about sawing wood!' The fact is that the same discipline that made it possible for me to keep my mind on other things while I was in prison enables me to block out the experience now. I really do sleep soundly." Not, of course, that blocking it out was the healthy thing to do in the long run.

MY RETIREMENT DATE was June 30, 1980, twenty years and six days after my enlistment in the Navy, and the question came up of using the occasion and my symbolic status as the first POW in North Vietnam for some sort of public affair. I didn't want it. In the climate of the times I just wanted to slip away. My wife and friends—Bill Lawrence, an admiral who was superintendent of the Naval Academy at Annapolis, and Dick Stratton, operations office there—organized a party at the boathouse on the academy grounds. Fellow POWs flew in. It was great, but ahead were uncertain waters.

The day after I retired from the Navy I signed on as clerk in a patent law firm. Tammy started selling cosmetics out of the house so she could be with the children. We were running hard, and losing ground. What did brighten our lives that fall of 1980 was the election of Ronald Reagan. The Reagans had kept in touch with us through notes, telegrams, phone calls,

After four years of desk duty in Washington I retired from the Navy without fanfare in September, 1980. Friends gave me a party at the Naval Academy in Annapolis where Admiral Bill Lawrence, then the superintendent, presented me with a flag.

and we considered them personal friends. More important, we felt that Reagan would bring back pride to an America humbled by its citizens held hostage in Iran. On election night Tammy and I uncorked champagne to toast the future.

After that temporary high I had to face up to some hard facts. The other law clerks were also law students with degrees in science but they were in their late twenties or early thirties. The only people my age were partners. The associates I worked for were ten years younger than I was. They held me in a sort of awe, which made it uncomfortable, awkward. I also found the work tedious and boring. I'd had more than my quota of boredom, and even the possibility of making a lot of money didn't affect that. I can still remember going home one day after digging around in the firm's library and telling Tammy, "Here we are. I'm forty-two years old, retired from the military and starting out on the second phase of my life. We've got two kids. I don't know what I am going to do with my life, but I do know one thing. I'm *not* going to be a patent attorney."

Along with many POWs, some squadron mates on the U.S.S. *Constellation* at the time I was shot down in August, 1964, came to the party. Flanking me, from left to right, were Murray Fitzgerald, Dave Edwards, Howie Alexander and Ray Berg. Ray, who had become a Washington lawyer, had an important influence on my life.

New friends at my retirement party who would also help shape my career were Ken Tomlinson, then head of Voice of America and now editor-in-chief of *Reader's Digest*, and his wife on Tammy's right and Bill Schultz, now managing editor of Reader's Digest, and his wife on my left.

MEANWHILE, THERE WAS a feeling of excitement in the air of Washington with a change of party and administration. Having been given tickets to the inauguration, we were a part of it, and Tammy suggested that I look for a government job. I had never thought of going that route, and besides, what was I qualified to do?

A response to that question came from Kenneth Y. Tomlinson, now editor-in-chief of *Reader's Digest* but then a member of the magazine's Washington staff. Ken had interviewed me for *POW*, a book about our North Vietnamese prison experience by John G. Hubble, a *Digest* roving editor, and we had gotten along well. He proposed a lunch with him, William Schulz, his Washington boss and now a *Digest* managing editor, and someone else in the new administration. "You and Tom Pauken ought to have a lot in common," he said. "He's a Vietnam vet—in intelligence out there. Now he's director of ACTION in the White House. I'm sure he'll have ideas for you."

It was a lunch with conversation ranging far and wide over areas in which the new administration would want an infusion of new blood. One of these areas was the Peace Corps, for which Pauken's ACTION had responsibility. An archconservative, Pauken said that the organization was dominated by liberals, holdovers from the Kennedy Administration when it was founded. I knew next to nothing about the Peace Corps' political orientation except that I'd heard it was something of a headquarters for antiwar activity. What I did know was that there was a need for it, or at least something like it.

I told the people at lunch about Sundays in one of the prisons I was in in '65 or '66. It was possible for a while there to climb up to the top of the window, hang onto the bars and look out over the countryside. Sundays were quiet days. From my cell I could see in the distance a building under construction with people crawling all over it. I could hear them talking, laughing, singing. When I asked a guard what was going on he said, "Oh, it's just Sunday labor. Everybody donates a day." I was impressed. I kept wondering what they could accomplish with electricity, with equipment, with technical training. "I think people in the underdeveloped world could do wonders if we could help them with the tools and the training," I said.

"Well, why don't you do it?" Tomlinson asked. "They've already picked a Peace Corps director but they need a deputy. Why don't you go for that?"

"Who, me?"

"Why not?"

"I'm not qualified."

"You're an engineer with an advanced degree. And you're a Republican, aren't you?" one of them said.

I was startled. I couldn't recall ever having told any of these men my political preference. It was the first time that I learned that it was just assumed that you were Republican if you were a Vietnam vet with what they called hero status. I nodded.

"Good," Pauken said. "I'm not so sure about the lady who's getting the top job—Loret Ruppe. I've got to go but if you're interested, give me a call."

Tammy was all for it. On the Washington scale it was a big job, a policy position. It would need confirmation by the Senate. When I'd first put out feelers for a government job I certainly hadn't had any such expectation. I'd been thinking along the lines of my naval work, some sort of middle-management position with a civil-service rating of G-14 or G-15. But one gift to me from Vietnam was the willingness to take risks. It comes to you naturally when you have nothing more to lose. I put in a call to Pauken.

"I'm interested in the Peace Corps job. What do I do?"

"Glad to hear it, Ev. I'll put your name in. Do you have some support? Do you know anyone in Congress?"

"A couple of people."

"Know anybody in the administration?"

"I know President and Mrs. Reagan, and Nancy Reynolds. . . ."

I called Nancy Reynolds and told her the whole story. She was as enthusiastic as Tammy: "You'd be good in that job. Write Nancy. She loves you. Write and ask her if she'll support you."

I followed that advice. I don't know what Mrs. Reagan

wrote to Pauken & Co. but I don't doubt that it reflected the enthusiasm that comes through in the note that she wrote to me from Camp David:

Dear Ev—

I was so happy to get your nice letter—thanks so much.

I am *so* happy you wanted to be with us—and even happier that it's all come to pass, as I understand it. I can't think of anyone I'd rather put in a good word for than you! I know you'll be great.

Please give Tammy my best—and your cute children—

Hope to see you soon—and, by the way, I'm sure we'll need the prayers you mentioned—all of them.

Fondly,
Nancy

Like me, Mrs. Reagan was evidently still relatively innocent of Washington ways when she wrote that "it's all come to pass." True—within a couple of days of my letter to her I got my first phone call from the White House. Years later I read with relish and understanding an article in the Washington *Post* entitled, "If the phone rings and they tell you it is the White House calling, hang up," but at the time all hands in our house in Rockville were very excited. I was to report to White House Personnel for an interview. I put on my most sincere suit, and Tammy lined the boys up. "Just think," she said, "your father is going down to the White House."

Actually my appointment was not in the White House itself but on the second floor of the Executive Office Building, an old ark next door that once housed the Department of State. A man named Alex Armindarez took me into his office, glanced through the papers on his desk and said, "I see you are a candidate for Deputy Director of the Peace Corps. I know who you are, your recommendation is impressive, so it just struck me—how about a bigger job?"

"Like what?"

"They're in a mess at the Veterans Administration. They

The White House Is Calling   119

need a director and a deputy, either of them bigger jobs than this and more in your line. Why don't you let me put your name in the hopper?"

Well, I was running into veterans' issues all the time and I was developing some strong feelings about how my fellow Vietnam veterans were being treated. So I asked Alex, "What do I do?"

He scribbled an address on a piece of paper and handed it to me. "This is a law firm," he said. "I want you to come over there this afternoon and meet some people." When I got there Alex and an attorney named Bill Geimer and some others were on hand. Alex presented me as a good candidate for Administrator of the VA, a solution to a deadlock between two other people battling for the position. The others seemed to agree. "What we're going to do is start a campaign to get you some support. We've got to get some congressmen and senators," they said. As we went out Alex said, "Go to it, Mr. Alvarez. See who you can round up. And don't worry. You've already got the Peace Corps job but let's hold off on that. This is much bigger."

There followed a month of craziness such as I hadn't known since getting out of prison. In between law-clerking and going to law school I was writing letters and making phone calls. We were getting calls at home at all hours from "the White House" urging me to contact this person or that. What with the uncertainty and interruptions, Tammy's nerves were on edge. We started snapping at each other. At one point Alex suggested, "Why don't you ask the President for a letter?" I put in a call to Nancy Reynolds—against my better judgment.

"They want me to be head of the VA. What do you think?" I asked her.

"But I thought you wanted the Peace Corps?"

"That's what they were talking at the time...."

"Well," Nancy said, "what do *you* want?"

I thought and decided not to bother the Reagans. But in the middle of February I did do one thing to ease tensions at home. I quit my law-clerking job. I also decided that if nothing else, I was at least getting a good lesson in government; knowing the people in the White House wasn't quite the same thing as having political support. As we were getting down to the wire Alex suggested that I talk to Bill Ayers, another candidate for the top job at the VA, about my being his deputy. Not exactly music to my ears but . . . After a bit of trying I finally managed to reach Ayers on the phone. "Ah, Everett," he said. "Nice hearing from you. I tell you what,

By the time of my retirement our family had been augmented by Bryan, who seems to be the star of this scene at the kitchen table of the home we bought in Rockville, Maryland, when we moved east from Monterey. (*UPI Photo*)

why not give me a call a little later on. Goodbye, Everett."

I hung up, thinking, He put me away nicely, didn't he? But I still didn't give up until Tammy said one day, "Who cares if the White House calls?" That did it. I got into the car and drove into Washington to see Alex. Sitting in the same little office where this all started, I said, "Alex, I don't know where this thing is headed, but just let me go to work. Let me go to the Peace Corps."

CHAPTER IX

A Warrior at Peace

PRESIDENT KENNEDY SAID about the Peace Corps after his brother-in-law Sargent Shriver got it started in 1961, "I gave Sarge a lemon and he made lemonade." By the time I joined the Corps as deputy director in late February twenty years later the lemonade was turning sour. The Peace Corps was another victim of the polarization in thought and feeling brought on by the Vietnam War. Staffed by young idealists, it was a Washington headquarters for antiwar activity. At one point flags of the National Front for Liberation—the Vietcong we were fighting—were hung from its windows. Viewing them from the White House across Lafayette Park, President Nixon said dryly, "Those are Peace Corps kids over there, aren't they?" Incidents like this raised tempers to the point of hatred in the prowar faction, especially on Capitol Hill. They were still boiling in 1981. When we had our first gathering of Vietnam POWs shortly after my appointment was announced, I got no congratulations. In fact, one of my prisonmates as much as said, What are you doing in the Peace Corps—turning traitor?

The attitude inside the old Peace Corps building that sat adjacent to Lafayette park was one of anger and apprehension as we new political appointees came aboard. In the executive offices there was something like a wild wake. Drapes had been torn from the windows, wine spilled on the carpeting. To the victor go the spoils is the law of politics, and everybody knew that many of the Carter appointees were on their way out. Aware of President Reagan's conservative agenda, the volunteers and civil-service staff were afraid of a hundred and eighty degree turn in direction and probably very leery of me. For good reason, since as I discovered in my first meeting with the newly named director, Loret Miller Ruppe, changing the guard at the top would be my unenviable task.

From a family of wealth and prestige, Director Ruppe had a lot of social polish and political savvy. She was born into the Miller Brewing Company dynasty in Milwaukee and her father was a folk hero as one of the Four Horsemen of Notre Dame football. Her husband Philip, a Republican congressman from Michigan and a Budweiser heir, had lost his seat in the 1978 elections. As a nod to him and a reward for her support of Bush in the Michigan primaries and service as cochairman of the Reagan-Bush committee in Michigan, Mrs. Ruppe was given the top post at the Peace Corps. A White House press release said that she had "spent most of her life in volunteer efforts" and that she had "traveled extensively and shared ideals with past Peace Corps volunteers in many countries." It was evident from her résumé that the first part of the statement was true. She hadn't earned a college degree and had primarily been a mother and homemaker. As for her sharing ideals with the Peace Corps, this was what Tom Pauken, her nominal superior as head of ACTION, feared.

I was only dimly conscious of all this when I first reported to Mrs. Ruppe. I was glad to have this interesting job and unconcerned about its political ramifications. Pleasant and friendly, Mrs. Ruppe made it clear that her function would be to set policy and act as spokesperson for the agency and that mine would be to oversee the day-to-day operations. In other words, she would carry the flag while I kept the crew in line.

No division of responsibility could have pleased me more. It was a big leap from clerking in a law firm or even acting as a Navy procurement manager to overseeing a budget of approximately $100 million and a corps of some 5,000 volunteers in more than sixty stations around the world. No matter what my POW status supposedly said about me, I was not a right-winger. I had no preconceived plans to change the Peace Corps. My only agenda was to make it work as efficiently and effectively as possible.

By then I had been around Washington long enough to learn that an essential first step in taking over a job like mine was to be certain of having a few able and loyal allies close at hand. I had met a man named Dominick (Nick) Onorato whose credentials I found most impressive. An aide at one time to my friend Admiral Zumwalt, Nick had pursued a civilian career in government since his retirement in 1969. He was expert in computer systems and, luckily for me, was on the lookout for a new challenge after a seven-year stint of reorganizing the Public Health Services. He agreed to become, in effect, my deputy as assistant director for management.

By my code, a wise second step in assuming a new command is to do a lot of looking and listening. As we got to know our colleagues by doing this, Nick and I quickly concluded that we had run into what he called "a unique persona." Peace Corps volunteers were not like most people. By a large and significant proportion, they were dedicated, idealistic individuals who were willing to give up two or more years of their lives for the service. However paradoxical it might seem, the esprit de corps and service motif in the Peace Corps were not unlike those in the military. These people really, sincerely wanted to do something good, and we were motivated to help them. But we also concluded that providing this help would involve the challenge that Nick was looking for.

To put it bluntly, we found shoddy administration, shoddy personnel records, shoddy planning. These were the result of a kind of inbreeding. The administration was largely in the hands of ex-volunteers who had signed on for permanent jobs

The first order of business for a top level political appointee is to recruit a savvy and sympathetic assistant. When I joined the Peace Corps I found just such a person in Nick Onorato, a former Navy officer and seasoned civilian bureaucrat who was looking for new challenges. He would be by my side in and out of government for nearly ten years.

at headquarters when their field tours were done. They had on-the-job training but were something less than skilled managers. When the money ran out they went on spending even though it was illegal, not to mention rather irresponsible. There was no apparent evaluation, no measure of the differences that the Peace Corps programs were making. Recruitment and training were separate functions with inevitable mismatching. Nick took over the job of tightening up the budget and organizational structure while I concentrated on personnel and programs.

I had to be the bad guy and let some very able Democratic appointees go. But this new-broom part of the political process also enabled me to get rid of some who didn't belong in government regardless of party affiliation. Filling these jobs allowed us to recruit people with more technical expertise and managerial experience. Loret Ruppe was not politically vindictive, and we did retain a great many people from former administrations. Sargent Shriver himself remained a sort of shadowy presence, and the whole place retained a Camelot mystique. Director Ruppe, who did, indeed, "share ideals with past Peace Corps volunteers," seemed to sense that this mystique had a value in attracting new volunteers.

I made an effort to meet as many Peace Corps people as possible at gatherings in this country and abroad. At one of these, a brave person got to his feet and asked a question that I knew was in most of their minds: "Why are you, a man of war, working at the Peace Corps?"

"Basically, nobody likes war, least of all the people who fight it," I told him. "We're all working for peace. I think there are many ways of doing this, and there are many very different people interested in peace. The Peace Corps isn't the only agency for peace."

I don't know how well that went down, but I did feel that people gradually lost their mistrust of me. I certainly gained respect for them from what I saw and heard in the field. My first trip abroad took me to Tunisia. We went down along the Sahara line to a small village where two American couples were working. They lived in the same primitive huts as the local people. They had to breathe fine blowing sand night and day and continually sweep it from their huts. They had to lug water from the lone well in the village. There was electricity, though, and one wife was ecstatic because she had just received a refrigerator. A young man who worked at a facility for processing oats into grain that had been built by Germans was translating the maintenance instructions from German into Arabic so that the local people could run it themselves. The other man was trying to establish hedgerows against the shifting sand and show local farmers how to save water by using a drip-type irrigation by perforating a hose from the pumps in the right places to feed individual plants instead of flooding a whole row.

This was what I thought the Peace Corps should be doing. In fact, I was discovering that most of the grassroots programs, like most of the people, were very worthy indeed. There were some, however, that seemed to me out of line or useless. For example, one woman who directed the North African sector had been concentrating on promoting feminism and the liberation of African women. I was also doubtful about the large number of volunteers teaching English as a second language in places where hunger and disease were the overwhelming problems. There was a division within the Corps between those of us who thought that we should be concentrating on technical aid in solving primary problems and those who thought that we should maintain as large a "presence" as possible, no matter what the volunteers were doing. It was easier and cheaper to recruit and train English teachers than technical experts. An enthusiast for her organization and its mission, Director Ruppe wanted to do both by enlarging the budget, and I was the man in the middle between her and Budget Director David Stockman.

I tended to come down on the side of fewer, better trained volunteers. As Mrs. Ruppe's deputy I felt obliged to support her, but our divergence of views did make for tension between us, not to mention battles with David Stockman. We were able to effect some economies, such as closing down operations in countries like Chile and Malaysia where per capita income and living standards had risen significantly. And we were very much together on introducing a Caribbean Basin initiative, a new effort to combine the operations of the U.S. Agency for International Development (AID) and the Peace Corps.

The initiative was right up my alley. My second trip abroad had been to the Dominican Republic, where a lot of Peace Corps volunteers from around the Caribbean were brought together. Many of them cornered me and said, "Why are we here? We're not doing anything." But after I explained the new program they caught fire. Basically, it was to have the Peace Corps volunteers train local people in the use of the material supplied by AID. The object was to develop independent farmers and small business people. As I well knew from my POW experience, nobody can accomplish anything when they are desperately hungry. So where there was hunger the major effort would go into creating an infrastructure to supply food. The next step would be to work on sources of energy for clothing, housing, tools, transportation. If these basics existed or had been secured, the final step would be to arrange funding and expert advice for the development of businesses and farms.

Although young people in the field welcomed such thinking, the very influential Peace Corps alumni group, which included senior staff people, did not. To them, working hand in hand with any U.S. government agency was the ruination of the Corps. They saw the Peace Corps as something apart, as representatives of the American people rather than the U.S. government. This attitude had been strengthened during the Vietnam War when for many the motivation for volunteering had been either to protest or to evade the conflict. It just couldn't go on if we were to achieve the economy and effectiveness of an interagency cooperation. When the subject came up I would say, "Wait a minute, who's paying salaries here? We're an extension, an arm of the United States government whether you like it or not."

Through all of this I found myself undergoing an experience in personal growth. I was thrust into a wholly different intellectual and social environment from any I'd known. I was working with liberals, attending international events with high officials, pleading on the Hill for funds from powerful and often hostile members of Congress. When I went overseas I was a dignitary on level four of the U.S. government, and my visits occasioned embassy parties and meetings with heads of state. Being shy and introverted by nature, I had to work particularly hard at this part of the job. I'm not a natural at, for example, making small talk and working a room.

A sidelight. The White House had invited me to a dinner in

honor of Mrs. Marcos, then first lady of the Philippines, at one of the Watergate restaurants. It was black tie, table of ten. Loret Ruppe was at the head table with Mrs. Marcos and I was at a table with one of her top aides. We paid for our supper by listening to a very long, very boring speech by Mrs. Marcos on why her husband was important to the U.S. When it was over her aide said, "Would you like to meet Mrs. Marcos?"

"Sure," I said, and the aide led me over to where she was saying goodbye to people. It took him a while to get her attention, and when she looked our way, he sort of shoved me forward, saying, "Mrs. Marcos, I want you to meet—"

She didn't let him finish. Looking me up and down, she said, "Oh, yes, he was very helpful to us today—very helpful," and turned to leave.

She had obviously mistaken me for what she considered a hotel flunky. When the aide started after her I grabbed his arm and told him to forget it. Obviously I didn't.

Another incident had different overtones. It was an intimate but formal affair hosted by Loret Ruppe in a private dining room of the University Club for President Siega of Jamaica and a few of his officials. Tammy was seated where she had to make conversation with the president. Tammy reached for a subject that she thought might make common ground between them. Having a Syrian background, she had been interested to learn that Siega might be Lebanese. "Mr. President," she said, "I understand you're of Lebanese background." He gave her an icy look and turned away. Tammy doesn't take snubs from anyone lightly. When Loret and I saw departing guests to the door, leaving Tammy and Phil Ruppe behind, he seized the moment to ask her, very seriously and confidentially, "How does Everett feel about being Mexican?"

Tammy was startled, to put it mildly. Whatever your background, it was just part of a way of life in Pittsburgh, where she was raised. There was nothing to "feel" about it. Instead of answering she asked, "What nationality are you, Phil?"

"Czechoslovakian."

"Oh, Phil, that's wonderful," said Tammy. "Some of my

mother's maids were Slovaks and they were such hard workers . . ."

The Alvarezes strike again.

I was soon too involved with an important task at the Peace Corps to worry over such matters. Even before Mrs. Ruppe and I were picked for our jobs the outgoing director of the Peace Corps, Richard Celeste—later governor of Ohio— sounded a note that turned into a trumpet blast from the liberals on Capitol Hill. He warned against using the Peace Corps for intelligence work abroad. He had heard rumors from the Reagan transition team that this would be done in spite of the fact that separation from intelligence activity had been so strict for twenty years that present or former intelligence officers were barred by law from serving as Peace Corps officials. The appointment of Tom Pauken, an intelligence officer in Vietnam, as head of ACTION changed rumor to reality in the view of Sen. Alan Cranston of California, who introduced legislation to restore the Peace Corps' status as an independent agency rather than stay under the wing of ACTION, a loose grouping of volunteer agencies created during the Nixon administration.

The prospect of losing the Peace Corps, its largest and most prestigious agency, did not go down well at ACTION. But Loret Ruppe was delighted with the move. Which put me in the middle again. At one point Pauken called me on the phone and pointedly asked me to see that certain people were given certain Peace Corps posts.

"That's not my role, Tom. I can't do that. That's the director's function, her decision," I told him.

His response was that I was being *un-American*. I couldn't believe it. My staff people told me that they could hear me telling Pauken where to go in choice four-letter words. Some ACTION people never spoke to me again, and I was attacked in ultraconservative publications for not doing my job in cleaning out the Peace Corps. Frankly, I am proud of those attacks today.

My "reward" for loyalty was assignment to head the task force from the Peace Corps to meet with the ACTION people and work out the administrative details of the separation. I put the problem into Nick Onorato's hands and he took care of it. But I did take away a lesson about working in the Reagan administration from this dustup. When White House people used the President's name—"The President wants this," "The President wants that"—Ronald Reagan usually didn't know about the matter or care about it. He was running the government by delegating such functions to his triumvirate of Meese, Baker, and Deaver, and *they* were the people you listened to.

WHAT WITH a demanding job that involved much travel and trying to keep up with law school, a year passed rapidly. I was also losing precious time with my family, and by the spring of '82 I felt that the challenge had gone out of the job. Nick and I and the others we had recruited had done what we had to do. We'd set up a budget process, reorganized the personnel and administrative structure, brought in people from the outside who were experienced in these areas, got participation in the Caribbean Basin Initiative started, separated the Peace Corps from ACTION. I had only one commitment left to keep—a long-scheduled and promised visit to the Peace Corps' Pacific installations in May.

Knowing by then how slowly things can move in Washington, I decided before I left to put out feelers through the White House personnel office for a new assignment that might be more in line with my personal interests. A lot faster than I had anticipated, my White House contact called and suggested I see the administrator of the Small Business Administration, who was looking for a deputy. An accountant from San Jose, Jim Sanders had just taken over the SBA. When I called he sounded pleased at the prospect of working with a neighbor and set up an immediate appointment. The job seemed ideal from many points of view. I could capitalize on my management training and experience and probably my legal studies, too. There wouldn't be as much traveling or socializing. I would learn a lot about business in case I ever wanted to get into the private sector. But I was a little suspicious about how quickly the opportunity surfaced, and I was no longer naive enough to think that political jobs were handed out on the basis of professional qualifications alone.

Indeed, before the ACTION people stopped speaking to me I had been given an unwelcome insight into the machinations behind appointments. How unwelcome can be judged by my passionate feelings about ethnic matters. I was, as mentioned earlier, always proud of being a Mexican-American, while I was growing up in Salinas and in the service, but I never considered it an element in my relations with other people or my work. If we had let being Mexican or Italian or black or whatever matter while we were in prison, the North Vietnamese would have splintered our group. And believe me they tried, especially working on me and Fred Cherry, a black Air Force pilot. They wanted us to feed their propaganda machine with material about mistreatment as members of oppressed minorities. For me, at least, the concept of being a minority person had never been in my head. Both Fred and I maintained that we were Americans and proud of our country, under all pressure and against all temptation, and our fellow-captives accepted us as such. It is not a position from which I will ever retreat.

The kind of ethnic polarization that had taken place in America while I was away was boldly evident in the Chicano movement in California, and it was subtly evident in the kind of question Philip Ruppe, however inadvertently, put to Tammy. But I still wasn't aware of its true nature until the day I picked up the phone in my Peace Corps office and heard a voice of a man—let's call him Dr. Rivera—say in hushed tones, "Can you come on down here?" I knew that Rivera was in ACTION, which had offices on the lower floors of our building. When I got there I found a couple of other men, but Rivera led the meeting. He warned that the telephones might be tapped and suggested that we keep our voices low.

"We've been trying to get hold of you to show you around, introduce you to the right people," he began. When I said I didn't feel in need of that service he went on, "Well, we want to get some real good Hispanics in here. Do you know any?"

If that was the direction in which they were heading anyway, I thought that I would weigh in with a name that fit the adjectives. I remembered a Los Angeles businessman, Al Zapaca, who had hosted me on a visit there. He had been a White House fellow, a Green Beret in Vietnam and was politically inclined. The men at the meeting looked at each other and smiled at the mention of his name. "He's not acceptable," one of them said.

"What do you mean?" I asked.

"He's not one of us. He's from a different camp."

"Well, what camp are you?"

"We're for Governor Reagan."

"So is Al. He's a Republican. I know that—"

They interrupted to explain that Al would never meet the litmus test of having done certain things in California, and I said, "Neither would I."

"Ah, but you're different. Your name came down from a different level," Rivera said, looking toward the White House across the park.

"He's the only one I know," I said, and got out of there.

Despite that incident, I have kept up good relations with Dr. Rivera and his group. Brought to Washington during the Nixon years, he has had a long history of advising on Hispanic affairs during conservative administrations. For instance, he was recently instrumental in the new trade agreement with Mexico.

But the implications of that affair weren't lost on me, and the first question I asked when I sat down across the desk from Jim Sanders at the SBA was: "Jim, am I being considered for this job because I'm supposed to be Hispanic?"

"Yeah," he said. "But you're really qualified, Ev."

"Thanks, Jim, but I'm not interested."

I was so angry that I was ready to quit the whole government right then. Instead of going back to my office I went straight to the offices of the White House personnel group. I started to boil over to the man who had sent me to SBA, but he stopped me and led me into another office, where I was face to face with Helene Van Dam, the director of personnel. A handsome woman, she had been Governor Reagan's secretary in Sacramento and would later be his ambassador to Austria. "Tell her what you were telling me," my guide said.

"I was just sent over as a candidate for a job because I'm supposed to be Hispanic," I said. "I really resent that. I didn't spend eight-and-a-half years of my life as a prisoner of war because I was Hispanic. I didn't get beat up because I was Hispanic. I was an American fighting man."

I didn't give her a chance to reply. I turned and walked out of there and went back to my Peace Corps office. Minutes later my phone rang. "This is Helene Van Dam. I don't want you to feel the way you evidently do. You're one of us. We know you, the President knows you. Please don't think we were doing that because you are Hispanic. We don't think of you that way."

It would have been churlish not to accept such an apology and I did. Later I was able to say yes when she called again just before my trip abroad to ask me if I might be interested in moving to the Veterans Administration, where the administrative problems had begun making copy for the press. Her call raised my hopes at a time when I was going through a private crisis. That spring semester one of my professors at George Washington Law School had flunked me in his course because I had missed too many classes. It was my first real failure at anything I had tried and, I felt, a severe setback. For the moment it seemed all of the sacrifices Tammy and I had been making to get that law degree could be for nothing. I was really feeling down. Dean Potts thought that the professor's ruling was unfair, but, he explained, he could not overrule a professor. Because of my travel plans, doing makeup work in summer school was out. After a few hours of black despair, I made up my mind that I would somehow finish the course that I had started on and qualify as a lawyer at any cost.

As I told Mrs. Van Dam, I was in a mood to leave the Peace Corps and the government entirely to go back to square one in terms of our family's struggle unless I got a job that would also allow me to carry my academic load. Quite apart from my intense personal interest in veterans' affairs, working at the VA would also keep me in country most of the time, and any legal knowledge that I had acquired would be of more use than in the Peace Corps.

Still up in the air about my future, I set off on one of the most fascinating adventures of my life. I had crossed the Pacific before to Hawaii, Japan, the Philippines on an aircraft carrier, but I had never been to any of those exotic islands of the South Pacific. I had never even imagined that I would get a chance to visit them. Yet here I was headed for places with names like Fiji, Tonga, Samoa. Bad as the timing was, I was excited to be going.

First stop was Fiji, a collection of some 330 islands, many of them dramatically mountainous and forested. A republic and then a member of the South Pacific Forum, Fiji had 800,000 people, three languages—Fijian, Hindustani, English—and three religions—Christian, Hindu, and Islam. The airplane had brought the islands into the twentieth century—but not by much. We would hop from island to island on single-engined, ten-passenger planes of New Zealand Airlines. Terminals were thatch-roofed shacks. Grass-skirted passengers, male and female, would board with crates of live chickens in hand. The landing fields were open spots of grassy hillsides that had been used in World War II. There was no copilot on any flight. I would sit in the copilot's seat and try to remember my basic flying in case of emergency. I'm glad none arose. I could see that landings and takeoffs took special skill. The pilot would come in from the ocean and land going uphill. After loading and unloading at the thatch terminal he would taxi to the middle of the strip, stand on his brakes while he revved up the engines and then race down straight for the ocean until he got enough airspeed to lift off.

A visit from a person of rank—mostly anyone with a job title—was almost an historic occasion in those far reaches of the Pacific. In Fiji I was called "Deputy Director of the Peace Corps of the World" and treated accordingly. It could turn a man's head. At every village we visited I had to participate in the ceremonies of hospitality, which basically consisted of sitting in a circle of elders on straw mats and tossing off bowls of a liquid made by mixing the powder from kava root with water. It had to be down the hatch—no sipping. The instant result was like having your mouth paralyzed by a strong shot of novocaine. I felt obliged to say something like, "That's good," which only brought another bowl. For a non-drinker like myself survival with at least some dignity intact was a real feat. But, seriously, the people were wonderfully friendly and generous. The highest gift they could give was a whale's tooth, and I'm proud to say I came away from Fiji with two of them.

On to Tonga. An independent kingdom with a monarch named Taufa'ahau Tupou IV, Tonga spread out over 150 islands, thirty-six of which were inhabited by little more than 100,000 people. There were two languages—Tongan and English—but a wealth of religions—Free Wesleyan, Roman Catholic, Free Church of Tonga, Mormon, Church of Tonga. An ingathering of some ninety Peace Corps volunteers from surrounding islands was planned at the capital of Nuku'alofa, and I was scheduled to stay for a week to meet them. As always, it was fun to be with these enthusiastic young people. I stayed in a hotel that looked like something out of *Rain* and we had picnics and parties. But the staged highlight was the night that the Peace Corps staff people and I were feted at a dinner in the home of the crown prince, a bachelor who loved to party. His father, the king, was a mammoth man, and the Prince was quickly catching up. His size gave him an almost inhuman capacity for alcohol. During the first round of drinks the prince learned that I had been a fighter pilot and insisted that I sit by him. Educated in England, he was fairly sophisticated about military aviation and very interested. He didn't want to talk about the Peace Corps at all and kept focused on me and what I could tell him about being a fighter pilot. This went on and on through rounds of drinks, through dinner, through more rounds of drinks. Many in the party were, understandably, nodding off.

At about 2:00 A.M. the still lively prince threw a chill into us all. "I tell you what," he said, "we're going to order up another case of whiskey."

Which was too much for Scott Hardman, the Peace Corps director, who threw diplomacy to the winds. "Your Highness, the wife of one of my staffers is ill and I must take her home. I'll take Mr. Alvarez back to his hotel, too."

"But the party's just getting started," the prince protested. "You leave Alvarez with me, take her home and come back."

"I can't do that, Your Highness. He has an appointment with your father in the morning and needs sleep . . ."

We almost had to back our way out, arguing the whole way as politely as we could. After we dropped the others at their homes we had to drive back by the prince's home. "If he sees

One of the pleasures of serving with the Peace Corps was the opportunity to see exotic places and meet fascinating people. Here I am with the King of Tonga, one of the Pacific island countries I visited in the summer of 1982.

us coming he'll insist we come in," Scott said, and turned out the lights and tried to slip by in the dark. No such luck. A booming voice sounded: "All right, I see you Hardman! Get back here!" Luckily for me Scott had the guts to keep going. It was all too soon and my head was throbbing when he came by again the next morning to take me to my audience with the king. Well, at least I had survived another of the hazards of serving my country.

After an uneventful stop in Western Samoa, where Robert Louis Stevenson is buried, I went on to the Philippines. I had just nodded off the first night when the phone rang. It was my Washington office telling me to call Helene Van Dam in the White House right away. When I got through, she told me, "We want you back here."

"I'll be back in two weeks—" I said.

"That's too long. We want you *now*. Things are breaking up at the VA and we want to get you nominated for the deputy's job before anyone knows it's going to be open and we get into a contest for it. Get yourself on the next plane."

It sounded like orders to me. At six o'clock the next morning I was on a plane bound from Manila for the United States. Two days later I was nominated for the post of deputy administrator of the VA.

When I told Loret Ruppe about it she graciously said, "It's a big job, good luck." I appreciated that.

CHAPTER X

Inside the Washington Wonderland

WHILE I WAS at the Peace Corps my alma mater Santa Clara University awarded me an honorary Doctor of Public Service Degree, but I didn't really earn it until I moved over to the Veterans Administration. President Harry Truman took an even sourer view of the job of running the VA than President Kennedy did of the Peace Corps. When Truman appointed Gen. Omar Bradley to the post of VA administrator, a colleague protested that it should have gone to a good Democrat. "I wouldn't do that to a good Democrat," said Truman. At my own confirmation hearings Sen. Alan Simpson, Republican of Wyoming and chairman of the Senate Veterans Affairs Committee, commented: "You were a prisoner of war? Why in the world would you want to take on a job like this?" In the next few years I would discover he had a point.

In theory, at least, a deputy's job is invisible, unimportant, and relatively simple. Not so with this one. The administration of the VA was in deep turmoil. The administrator Robert P. Nimmo had been in office less than a year and two deputies had already resigned to protest his methods. In addition, Nimmo was being charged with appropriating government property for personal use, specifically an automobile and furniture for his daughter's office. With the media's cameras focused on him he was almost certain to be out of office in a matter of months. At issue within the walls of the VA building at 810 Vermont Avenue and out on the streets sprouting angry demonstrations was the treatment of Vietnam veterans.

Whether true or not, many Vietnam veterans perceived Nimmo and the VA's civil service staff—almost all of World War II vintage—as being indifferent or hostile to their concerns. According to them, the attitude of old-timers at the VA was "We won our war, what's wrong with you guys?" Those who served in Vietnam felt that they were looked on as

In the same month that I visited Tonga, I returned to my alma mater, the University of Santa Clara in California, to receive an honorary Doctor of Public Service degree. I would really earn it in my next job at the Veterans Administration. While Father Rewak read the citation, my very good and influential friend Jim Shea fussed with my hood.

It certainly helped at my August, 1982, Senate confirmation hearings for the post of Deputy Administrator of the Veterans Administration to be introduced by a fellow POW, Senator Jerry Denton, Republican from Alabama.

Senator Alan Simpson, Republican from Wyoming, who headed the Veterans Affairs Committee holding my confirmation hearings, asked from his seat in the center of this picture why I'd want to take on such a job after all I had been through. It turned out to be a perceptive question.

grubby characters, losers and loafers in need of a shave and a haircut, drunks and druggies. In what was developing into the hottest veterans' issue of the century—the possible after-effects on military personnel of the use of Agent Orange to defoliate the jungles in Vietnam—the VA was charged with sitting on its hands. Action was obviously in order to change both the image of the VA and that of the Vietnam veteran. Like my disillusioned predecessor as deputy, Vietnam vet-eran Charles T. Hagel, Jr., my job would be to represent the interest of my comrades in arms.

I knew this wouldn't be easy, but it was a strong motivation for taking on the job. Much of the protesting by Vietnam veterans was done right in my front yard at the Peace Corps—in Lafayette Park, where they could be seen from the White House. On occasion when I walked through the park I would invite one or two disgruntled veterans to join me in a cup of coffee at the cafeteria in our building. I would listen to their complaints, many of which seemed justified. I was already aware of the disparity between the treatment we POWs had been accorded as heroes and the neglect or downright scorn accorded the average grunt. This was manifestly unfair. Whatever I could do to use my so-called hero status to right some of this wrong would be worth whatever it took.

Quite apart from current issues and problems, any top executive at the VA would have to contend with the vexa-tions that Harry Truman foresaw back in 1945. The VA had become the largest independent agency in government. In my time there were 235,000 employees, 79,000 volunteers, 172 medical centers, 226 outpatient clinics, 100 national cemeteries, 135 veteran outreach centers and a budget of more than $25 *billion*. With a constituency of 30 million vet-erans, whatever the VA does affects the lives of at least 100 million Americans. The VA's policies and practices play a crucial role in the whole medical and welfare system of the country. Operating this immense agency is not—and never will be—just a matter of good management. Anything having to do with veterans is highly politicized. Potentially their votes can make or break a congressman, and possibly a presi-

In keeping with that family tradition, Tammy brought the boys to the confirmation hearings. Behind her right shoulder is Nick Onorato, who would move with me from the Peace Corps to the VA.

dent, and they are represented in Washington by powerful organizations with highly skilled lobbyists.

I got the political message in the few days between arriving back from the Philippines and the announcement of my nomination. I was summoned to the White House to pass muster by the executive directors of the three largest veterans groups—Mylio Kraja of the American Legion, Cooper Holt of the Veterans of Foreign Wars, and "Gabby" Hartnet of the Disabled American Veterans. These were the powerhouses in Washington, the people who called the agenda about veterans' issues. They didn't like what was going on at the VA. They had considered Hagel their champion and were upset by his resignation. The story was that Hagel had put it bluntly to the White House: either Nimmo went, or he would go. The President chose to keep Nimmo, an old California friend and supporter. Where did I stand?

That question was more in their minds than on their lips. At the meeting they mostly looked me up and down, not saying much, letting me talk. I told them that I thought I understood veterans' issues since I was a veteran myself and had been through more than most of them had. They were cautious. "Well, we'll wait and see how you do," one of them said.

Because of the veterans' political clout, the VA had had little trouble getting what it wanted until the Reagan administration arrived in Washington. Its concept of having a

One of my first duties at the VA was to explain my agenda to a gathering of executives from the nation's veterans groups.

I collected hard hats, too, during very essential inspections of facilities under construction. Here, I was looking over the site of a new hospital in Portland, Oregon, in 1983.

leaner, meaner government was meant to apply to the VA, too. Within an hour of moving into my tenth-floor office, I knew squaring this with veterans' needs would be my major responsibility. My first meeting with Bob Nimmo was short but staggering. A polite and personable man, he had little to say, and it was obvious that he had personal problems on his mind. "It's yours. You run the agency," he told me in almost those exact words.

"What do you want me to do?" I asked.

"Whatever you like. Whatever seems right to you," he said.

Fortunately I had again been able to persuade Nick Oronato to come along with me this time and take the job of associate deputy administrator for information-resources management. He would again be my right hand. I needed a left hand as well, and I decided to use that need as a device to bridge a yawning gap in the VA structure. There was no regular contact between the top echelon of political employees on the tenth floor, who lived, as it was said, "behind the glass doors," and the career civil servants who staffed the agency's operating divisions. Basically there were three of these—the medical department that operated the hospitals and clinics, the benefits division that took care of loans, pensions, rehabilitation programs; and the memorial department that managed the cemeteries. The professionals, some of whom had been in the VA for as long as forty years, viewed the politicals with distrust and disdain. So for my left hand, my executive assistant, I examined the rolls of the professionals and picked Leo Wurschmidt, a young ex-Marine who had established a good record in all three operating branches during an eight-year VA career.

Learning that my predecessors had seldom met with the heads of the medical, benefits and memorial staffs, I brought them all together and said, "Look, I think we ought to meet periodically—like every morning. Let's organize ourselves. I want to know what's going on. Let's make these meetings brief—bring up the subjects, discuss the issues and who's taking care of what, then back to your own staff and on with the day."

The system worked well. I tried to keep the meetings from getting stuffy or argumentative. We all have a built-in instinct, as strong as in any animal, to protect our home turf. People in large bureaucracies, whether in or out of government, get particularly good at it. This was true of the medical department of the VA. It was very complex—by design. The harder it was to understand it, the harder it would be for anyone to criticize it. They had a huge budget and a group of budget analysts who were evasive, illusive—wizards in laying down a statistical smokescreen. When there was a point under discussion that these budgeteers had fuzzied up I wouldn't get angry. I'd walk over to my window where there was a radiator with a duct leading down through the building. I'd lean toward the duct and yell, "Hey, you down in the budget shop, you down there on the sixth floor. Screw you. We're onto you." I don't think they ever heard me down there, but the people in the meeting did—and while they were laughing got the point about communicating instead of covering up.

I was learning then—and hope I'm still learning—that the medium of a little humor helps get the message across. I suspect, for example, that my confirmation hearings for the

All political appointees serve the administration in power, and meetings like this with the top man are one of the privileges of this service. Looking on is Bob Nimmo, head of the VA when I came aboard, who resigned and left me in the role of Acting Administrator for a few months. (*Official White House Photograph*)

VA post made the wire services as much because of a quip as because of all the nice things my fellow POWs said about me, including Jerry Denton, who was then a senator from Alabama. I recalled that the hearing was taking place exactly eighteen years after, and almost exactly at the same hour of, my shoot-down. "I hope lightning doesn't strike twice," I told the senators. When I appeared on Larry King's show he asked me, "What is it like being shot down?" My instinctive response was to look up to the heavens and say, "It tends to ruin your day." Starting off with a smile makes it easier to do serious business.

In the way of supposedly serious business, I was called upon to attend my first cabinet meeting in Nimmo's place in the fall of '82. I tried to keep calm and pretend it was routine as I walked over to the White House and through the door to the West Wing, where the Cabinet Room is located. I wasn't too successful. When I edged into the room and saw the people taking their seats—Meese, Deaver, Baker, Secretary of State George Shultz, Secretary of Defense Casper Weinberger—I kept thinking, *If the folks in Salinas could only see me now!* They'd never believe it. I took a seat at one end of the table next to Secretary of Housing and Urban Development Samuel R. Pierce, Jr., who would become famous as "Silent Sam." President Reagan sat in the center with his back to the long row of windows looking out on the Rose Garden; Vice President Bush sat across from him.

On the agenda was a presentation by Joseph Wright, a deputy to Budget Director David Stockman. He was going to explain an innovative program called Reform 88. The result of a very complex effort, it was intended to eliminate waste, reduce paperwork and generally increase government efficiency. A banker by profession, Joe was slim and wiry with dark brown hair greying at the temples, a businessman to the core. Aware of the President's impatience with detail, Joe had reduced his complicated subject to a snappy, twenty-minute slide show. Behind the Vice President, he had set up a projector at one end of the table and a screen at the other. With a slide of Reform 88 on the screen, Joe got off to a good start. But when he flipped the slide, the next one was out of sequence.

"Sorry, Mr. President, this isn't the slide you want to see, but the next one will be," Joe said confidently.

Click. The next slide was upside-down. Joe kept talking about his concept. Click. Something was wrong with the third slide, too. Prancing back and forth and fussing with the projector, Joe kept talking, and the slides kept coming up wrong. He was losing his audience.

I saw President Reagan start looking around, up and down the table, out of the windows. There were two or three jars of jellybeans on the table. The President reached for one, took a handful capped the jar and slid it over to the Vice President.

The Vice President helped himself and slid the jar back to Ed Meese. All of a sudden, all of the jelly bean jars were sliding back and forth across the table. Even Secretary Pierce and I got some. Notes were passing, too, and there were suppressed giggles. All the while, Joe was frantically clicking his out-of-synch slides and talking away.

President Reagan picked up a carafe of water, poured himself a glass and sent that shooting across to Vice President Bush. As he raised the glass to his lips, the President said, "This smells like gasoline. I swear there's gas in this . . ."

"What? What?" somebody said in alarm, and across the table somebody else took the top off the carafe, whiffed and said, "Hey, it does smell like gas. Like kerosene." Somebody opened another carafe and said, "This one smells like gas, too . . ."

Of course, there wasn't any gas in there. But with that, the President stood up from the table and walked away. Bush followed him. Everybody else started to leave while talking to each other, ignoring poor Joe who kept speaking in the background. I turned to Sam Pierce and said, "Holy smokes!" I went to many more cabinet meetings that were serious and productive, but I was never again in awe of the others at the table. From the top down, they were very human beings.

As PREDICTED, Nimmo resigned in early October of '82. The top job was again up for grabs. Since I was already the functioning head of the agency I thought I maybe had a reasonable chance of getting the appointment. So did the newspapers that put me among the viable candidates. It didn't happen. The President reached out to Harry N. Walters, a New York State businessman who had been rewarded for his campaign efforts by appointment as an assistant secretary of the Army. An all-American fullback on coach Red Blaik's famed "lonely end" team at West Point, Walters had served four years in the Army after his graduation in 1959 before opting for a business career. He was and is an energetic, charismatic man, a military booster who later organized the great Washington welcome for the Gulf War troops. My seesaw life had taught me to take downers in stride, and my military service had taught me to serve the person placed in command over me. Soon after his appointment was announced I went over to Harry Walters's home and told him that I would do my damndest to be a good deputy to him, and we shook hands on it.

There was, though, one aspect of the affair that did upset me. The VFW's Cooper Holt was quoted as saying, "Alvarez will never get it. They have to have a WASP in that job." I thought that I had laid the issue of my background to rest when I was at the Peace Corps. But Ambassador Van Dam had departed for Austria, and it began rearing its unlovely head again. I kept shoving it down. In a typical instance I got a call from the White House's Office of Public Liaison. One of the men there who dealt with Hispanics said, "Everett, we want you to fly on Air Force One with the President to Texas."

"When?" I asked.

"Tomorrow morning. We want you on the podium down there with Mr. Reagan."

I knew nothing about the issues in Texas, and I had a briefing scheduled on the Hill. "Sorry, I'm busy tomorrow," I said and hung up.

Minutes later John Harrington, who replaced Helene Van Dam as head of the White House personnel office, was on the phone. "John, I'm busy, I'm not going to go," I said.

"Do you know anyone else?"

"No. What's this all about?"

Since this was the same man who once told me that he was surprised that I spoke such good English, I wasn't surprised when he said bluntly, "They're looking for a token Hispanic to go along."

I was more seasoned another time when a different man in Public Liaison called about six o'clock of an evening and caught me just leaving the office. "Hey, Everett, we want you to represent President Reagan at a ceremony in Rhode Island."

"When is it and what is it?"

"Tomorrow morning. They're turning over two destroyers to the Mexican Navy."

Real subtle.

"I'm busy, I have an important speech of my own tomorrow somewhere else," I told him, boiling inside. "Why don't you call me when they're launching a new carrier? But don't call me for this sort of thing anymore."

The Mexican Navy? When I calmed down it reminded me of the needling that went on among men in sports, in the service, in prison. "Here comes the Mexican Navy," was one of the things they would throw at me, but I would throw it right back. I've always thought that there is something wrong with people who can't take that kind of kidding as part of camaraderie. But being paraded as a token was something else. I guess I made my point on the phone, because I didn't get any more such requests after that.

Like Loret Ruppe, Harry Walters designated me chief operating officer of the agency while he would act as spokesman outside and inspirational leader inside. Perhaps because we had different styles—mine has been called laid-back, his flamboyant—we complemented each other.

We also agreed on the agency's mission: to serve the veteran, and that the best way to do that was to get out from behind those glass doors on the tenth floor and motivate the career people who were actually delivering the services.

I had started the process with my daily briefings of department heads, but with Harry aboard we carried it much further. Beginning with that first Christmas, for example, he and I would split up the eleven floors of the building and visit every office to give holiday greetings to each of some 3,000 people. What I tried to project to staffers around the country as well as in Washington was that I was somebody who might not always agree with them but who would always listen. We wanted this same message to go out to the public. One way was a monthly administrator's award presented with ceremony to the staffer who wrote the best letter of response to some veteran's inquiry. No big deal. Little things like that cost nothing, but they did pay off. Today, ten years later, some of my brother-in-law's patients who work at the VA talk about the high morale that was there during those years.

The annual battle of the budget was fierce, and it was one that Harry and I fought together. The first round was always with the green eyeshade people in David Stockman's Office of Management and Budget who dealt in numbers rather than the impact of programs they funded. Harry and Stockman were antithetical personalities, and their "discussions" could turn into shouting matches. There was a point where they reached a real deadlock. Unless some of OMB's cuts in the VA budget were restored, Harry wouldn't support the President's budget on the Hill. The argument was adjourned to the White House, where Meese and Baker tried to mediate. Harry and David sat glaring at each other until Jim Baker finally asked, "What is it that you *really* need?"

Harry turned to me. "What is it that we really need, Ev?"

I got out my shopping list of what we wanted and read it off. Astute politicians that they were, Meese and Baker agreed to most of it. As we gathered up our papers to leave, my counterpart Joe Wright said to me, "Ev, I've heard of cleaning out the store, but couldn't you at least have left the shelves?"

The second round of the budget battle would take place on Capitol Hill. It was like wrestling on a slippery floor. Members of Congress themselves seldom have the time or interest to delve into the details of budgets for huge organizations like the VA or Department of Defense. They leave that to their staffers, who in turn rely heavily on lobbyists for information and guidance. Our own people in the bureaucracy would also lobby Congressional staffers behind our backs to get more money for their particular project. So the footing was always uncertain when you appeared before a committee that might be misinformed or even misled.

One case in point. While we had a major study under way to determine how many hospital beds were needed for veterans in Florida I was called to testify before a House subcommittee on hospitals and health-care systems. The members apparently thought that we were going to ask for an additional $200 million to build a hospital in the West Palm Beach area. It was news to me. Where did they get it? One of them held a copy of our own VA study. It had been passed to Congressional staffers by VA staffers before it reached those of us on the tenth floor. The study did, indeed, recommend building a new hospital. A local congressman had already been flying people down to look at sites in his district. The study as such wouldn't have gotten beyond my desk, or Harry's either, if it had stayed in channels. It was based on outmoded methodology and contained no alternatives such as leasing existing facilities. Not surprisingly, incidents like that made it hard to sell people on our legitimate needs.

To be as sure as possible that I would be on solid ground in selling those needs, I got out around the country to inspect

Another continuing duty was making speeches, and it began at my swearing-in ceremony. Hopefully, I had improved since my early efforts in Monterey.

I still have an office full of shovels left over from the many ground-breaking ceremonies at which I participated, like this one for a new VA facility in Memphis in 1983.

Heart-to-heart talks with influential men like Al Keller, National Commander of the American Legion, were essential to learn what our VA constituency wanted.

installations and meet our people as often as I could. I made my first visit to a hospital in the Bronx in New York before I was sworn in and came away with a mixed bag of feelings about the job I'd just taken on. The hospital was not new but it was in the process of being rebuilt section by section. In a facility that you had to enter through a metal detector to make sure you weren't carrying a knife or gun, I was introduced to Dr. Rosalyn S. Yalow, a researcher who had shared a Nobel Prize in 1977 for her work in body chemistry. Right there in one spot I was seeing medical service delivered to some of our most desperate and disadvantaged citizens and basic research support being provided for the whole world health-care system. It was inspiring. But I also saw something puzzling that would draw me into a losing battle for years.

Right in the hospital's main entryway was a multicolored, conical piece of modern artwork rising two stories to the ceiling. The director referred to it offhandedly as "our monstrosity" and explained that it was there because Congress had mandated that *ten percent* of the design-cost of hospital buildings be spent on art projects. The piece was certainly nonobjective. I'm frank to say I couldn't divine any meaning or beauty in it. But while we were crossing a courtyard to meet Dr. Yalow the director pointed to a wall decorated with a bright mural. "Look at that," he said. "Nice, isn't it? We paid a million for that monstrosity back in the lobby, and the kids in the neighborhood painted that wall for free."

Back in Washington, I dug into the bowels of the VA and found an office occupied by a woman whose responsibility was to manage the "Art in Architecture" program. I asked for a scrapbook of pictures of all of the art projects in place or being planned. I also began paying attention to them when I made visits or reviewed plans. At a new nursing home in Chicago the director led me to an inner courtyard containing an object that resembled a giant cheese slicer and gave vent to his feelings by saying, "Just look at *that* damned thing!" On the plans for another nursing home in Butler, Pennsylvania, was a work of art that consisted of blocks piled at crazy angles as if about to fall over. When I asked the director about it he said, "Oh, don't worry, we'll stick it out back where nobody can see it." By contrast, I noticed an exciting bronze statue of Audie Murphy in battle dress at the hospital named for him in San Antonio, Texas, and discovered that local veterans groups had donated it. In a state veterans home at Kings Point, Wisconsin, there was an impressive figure of a World War I doughboy provided by *public* subscription.

Why were we installing at great expense art work that people didn't like or want while other institutions were getting art at no government expense that pleased people? In my view it had something to do with the selection process. Our mandated art work was chosen by a committee of the National Endowment for the Arts, and their choices tended to favor the work of avant garde artists. Showing my scrapbook around, I began to propose that we at least open up the competition more and have representatives of the VA and veterans groups involved in the judging process. What I opened was a can of worms. I got calls from the NEA and their supporters in the Congress and the press. I would point out that on a $180 million project the architectural fee would be $18 million, of which $1.8 million would go to Art in Architecture. With so many hospitals out there underequipped and understaffed I could do a lot with that amount of money. I was not encouraged to proceed with my idea, and the art program continues.

On the whole, though, I felt that I was winning more battles than I was losing. With the backing of Harry Walters and the help of my right and left hands, we made real inroads in the VA's antiquated communications and accounting systems. In the aftermath of the catharsis provided by the building of the memorial wall, as told in the prologue of this book, we made fast strides in integrating Vietnam vets into the system. We hired them to work in the VA itself as places opened up. We reached out to them in the streets by expanding a storefront-counseling program, started by my predecessors, from fifteen to nearly 200 installations.

Looking back, I'm sometimes more pleased by the things I

Nothing is more important in running a government agency than good relations with the powerful people on the Hill. Harry Walters, my boss as the Veterans Administration's Administrator, and I rubbed shoulders often with Congressman Sonny Montgomery, Democrat from Mississippi, Chairman of the House Veterans Affairs Committee.

didn't do than those I did. In a politically sensitive job it's easier and usually more self-serving in the long run to say yes rather than no. My toughest tests at the VA came when I had to say no to two fellow POWs. Jerry Denton, the Republican senator from Alabama who had testified eloquently in my behalf at my confirmation hearing, called one day and said, "Ev, can you do me a favor and have your people look at the Providence Hospital in Mobile? It's a nice hospital run by some nuns but I think they're in a position to be taken over. I just want to be able to say that the VA is taking a look at it."

"Sure, Jerry, we're always doing that," I said truthfully.

The VA tried to be alert to facilities that would lend themselves to conversion since it was so much cheaper than building. Nine times out of ten, however, our scouting teams

I frequently traveled around the country to represent the VA, as on this occasion when both Governor Dukmejian and I spoke at the Veterans Home of California in 1984.

I was also a speaker at one of the first of the annual POW-MIA recognition events that are held all over the country. This one was in Chicago.

would report back that there was too much work to be done in the way of renovation to make a takeover feasible. This was the one in ten—a nice hospital, in good shape. I couldn't lie to Jerry about the report, but I had to tell him that there was one big hitch: the VA didn't need a hospital in Mobile. Under the prodding of Sonny Montgomery, a Democrat of Mississippi and chairman of the House Veterans Affairs Committee, we had just renovated a hospital in Biloxi that was intended to serve the Mobile area forty miles away across the state line as well as Biloxi. Jerry, a Republican senator, couldn't take that lying down, and there developed a battle royal between him and Sonny with me in the middle. I stood my ground, and, sorry to say, Jerry Denton lost his seat in the Senate.

The other case was less dramatic but no less difficult for me. When the patient load dropped in the surgical wing of the VA hospital in Prescott, Arizona, we decided that the veterans would be better served by shutting down the surgical wing and helping them find care elsewhere. Although Arizona senator John McCain, another Republican and staunch POW, didn't personally put any heat on me, I knew that our decision would be politically damaging to him. So I was particularly touched when Senator McCain said later of the incident: "The definition of courage according to Ernest Hemingway is grace under pressure. I have seen Ev Alvarez display that both in and out of prison. As deputy director of the VA he was sometimes under enormous pressures. One of these times was when he had to close the surgical ward of the VA facility in Prescott. He was very calm, very deliberate. In response to the pressure he ordered the closing to be restudied. It was restudied with the same conclusion. Then he stood steadfast."

The hottest issue that Harry and I had to handle was Agent Orange. To some extent the charges by Vietnam vets that the VA was sitting on its hands about Agent Orange were true. Although there were studies going on in the Air Force, the Department of Defense, the VA itself, nobody had come up with clear evidence of the connection, if any, between Agent Orange and the ailments or diseases that the Vietnam vets claimed had been caused by their exposure to Agent Orange. Since we couldn't read it their way, the Vietnam veterans claimed that the VA was exhibiting another of its anti-Vietnam stances. But as Harry and I looked at the matter we decided it was—in Harry's football parlance—one ball we shouldn't be carrying. Whatever decision we reached could be seen as biased or politically motivated. So we arranged through legislation to pass the ball to the world's leading epidemiologists at the Center for Disease Control. The VA would put up sixty-five to seventy million dollars to fund a truly rigorous seven-year study. Meanwhile we at the VA would offer priority medical care to any Vietnam veteran for any illness that he or she believed resulted from Agent Orange. This didn't get rid of the controversy. What many of the veterans wanted was something beyond our power to give—money.

JUGGLING THE RESPONSIBILITIES of the job with the demands of family and personal life in those times was hard, but Tammy and the boys have been nice enough to say I did it well. I can only say I tried. I find it hard to believe now that I managed to get back in the good graces of the law school, thanks to Dean Potts and my writing special papers in the fall of '82, and that I carried my courses until I passed the final exams in February, 1983. I gave myself two years of intermittent study before I tackled the D.C. bar exams, which I passed in '85.

During this time, whenever I appeared in public Tammy, Marc and Bryan were likely to be found somewhere out in the crowd. I was known around Washington for a picture in the paper of me on my knees tying my son's shoe while Lyn Nofziger, President Reagan's aide, waited to swear me in as deputy to the Peace Corps. My fellow workers knew me for sometimes walking out of important meetings to attend some emergency or, more important to me, at least, an event at home. The travel and social side of the VA job wasn't as demanding as it had been in the Peace Corps. But even so, we decided that it was more important for Tammy to stay home

Taken in the White House and published in the Washington *Post*, this picture of Presidential aide Lyn Nofziger waiting patiently to swear me in as Deputy Director of the Peace Corps while I tie Marc's shoelace became symbolic of my priorities in life—family first.

with the children than to accompany me to most affairs—at some risk to what the British call "preferment" in a community, where after-hours socializing with spouses is often the grease of progress.

Harry Walters and I developed a relationship outside as well as inside the office. Our boys called the Walters Uncle Harry and Aunt Illa, and there was one occasion when Harry might have wished that we had kept things on a more formal level. On a family visit to the Walters' home, then seven-year-old Bryan was playing with the dog and calling it "him." Harry corrected him: "It's a she."

"How do you know, Uncle Harry?"

While Illa whispered, "Let's see him get out of this one," Harry rolled the dog over, pointed to the appropriate place and said, "There's no stick there—you know, like you have."

"Oh," said Bryan. Then a minute later, after some thought, he asked, "Uncle Harry, how do you tell if a cat's a he or she?"

"Same way, you roll it over and look."

After further contemplation, Bryan asked, "Uncle Harry . . . How do you tell a horse?"

"Same way, Bryan, you look . . . no stick, it's a she."

"No Uncle Harry, how do you turn the horse over?"

In 1984, though, there was an occasion too important for either of us to miss. I was asked to give the pledge of allegiance at the Republican National Convention in Dallas on the night that President Reagan would accept his renomination. Tammy agreed to leave the boys with their grandmother in Pittsburgh. Harry and Illa were on hand too, and we shared a suite with them on one of the two floors in the tower of the Loews Anatole Hotel. This was literally high living. We had to show special passes and go through metal detectors to use the special elevators to the towers, and it was possible to be stuck above or below for as long as half an hour if the President was using them.

Except for a metal detector holding up Tammy at the entrance to the hall on account of her gold-buckled belt and gold bracelet, embarrassing her no end, the evening went well, and after the ceremonies Tammy and I were invited by the Reagans to join them in a reception backstage. The faces were familiar. Bob Dole and his wife Libby, both of whom knew Tammy as well as they did me. Weatherman Willard Scott and his wife. Michael Reagan and his wife and children. George and Barbara Bush with a portion of their large family. Although he had met her only once before and then at a large gathering, George Bush made points with Tammy when he came over with singer Ray Charles. "Tammy," he said, "I'd like you to meet a friend of mine—my main man!" Tammy understood well what he meant by the phrase from her days in Pittsburgh when she mingled with jazz-loving friends. It was a relaxed night, a night of victory, and a night to remember.

Early the next morning I took a ride on Air Force One. Harry and I were invited along to be with the President as he spoke at a VFW convention in Chicago. Harry and I were whisked in a limousine entourage from our Dallas hotel to the Naval Air Station, where Air Force One was parked. After a flight to Great Lakes Naval Air Station we were picked up planeside by a helicopter and dropped right by the lake in downtown Chicago where a motorcade was waiting to rush us to the convention site. We followed the President in through a back way, stood on stage while he spoke, followed him back out to the helicopters and were soon on our way again to Washington. Changed into a comfortable sweatsuit, the President came back from his forward quarters for a chat with Illinois congressman Henry Hyde. Sitting beside Harry and me and knitting all the way without dropping a stitch was a young woman not then known to worldwide TV audiences as the State Department spokesperson—Margaret Tutwiler. Dick Darman, who would replace David Stockman as head of OMB, was quietly crunching numbers across the way. The flight, like the evening before, was something I'd long remember.

IT WOULD BE WRONG to say that my VA job ever became routine, but in the year after that Reagan sweep of '84, things did settle down some. There still were enough aggravations for the post to stay on Truman's unwanted list in the eyes of most people, but I was thoroughly enjoying the work because I

The most moving and memorable moments of my public career came during ceremonies to honor fallen comrades. Shown here during prayers on Veterans Day, 1982, at Arlington National Cemetery, I would later introduce Defense Secretary Casper Weinberger, standing to my left.

believed deeply in the cause—serving the veteran. How could I feel any other way when I kept running into spontaneous expressions of appreciation from the veterans? The most touching took place at Arlington National Cemetery on a Memorial Day. Standing in for my boss at the traditional ceremonies, I introduced Defense Secretary Weinberger. After the speeches a legless Vietnam veteran wheeled himself up to me, took my hands in his and kissed them. He was crying as he said, "Thank you, thank you, thank you, for all you're doing for us." I was never happier that I had already learned to cry again myself.

CHAPTER XI

"... to care for him who shall have borne the battle ..."

ALTHOUGH I HAVE BEEN out of uniform for a dozen years, in my heart I am still an American military person, Vietnam vintage. There are millions like me from all wars. They call us veterans. Wars end, but their effect on human lives does not go away. Abraham Lincoln understood this when he charged the American people "to care for him who shall have borne the battle, and for his widow and his orphan." While I was at the Veterans Administration I walked by those words on the wall by the main entrance and amended them in my mind by adding two words—"or her." Taking my inspiration from Lincoln seemed appropriate since the war he presided over was even more divisive than the war I fought in. Yet eventually the American people came to appreciate the courage and sacrifice of the fighting men on the Confederate as well as the Union side. They learned to separate the warriors from the war.

Long before this became a popular phrase during the Gulf War, it was the essence of what I preached and tried to practice. Although the physical wounds may be the same, the psychological wounds of bearing the battle can be worse for the warrior thrust into an unpopular or indecisive conflict. This was apparent in studies of veterans from both the Korean and Vietnam wars. The kind of pride that can help an individual plaster over the raw, wrenching experiences inevitable in warfare isn't there when a nation fails to honor a person's service. How we treat our veterans isn't just a matter of showing sympathy. How we treat our veterans is a matter of assuring that the nation will keep producing people with the conviction and character to bear its battles.

There are those who feel that the reception given the Gulf War veterans was overdone. I'm not one of them. I was for anything that would honor American troops because the re-

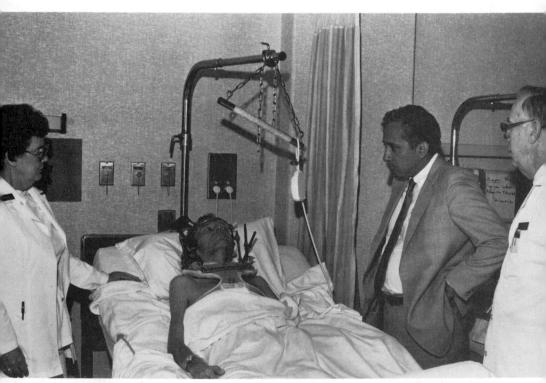

I felt that my function at the VA should be far more than ceremonial. Whenever I could, I visited the sick to learn of their problems and treatment firsthand.

At meetings of veterans, I always tried to be a good listener. Even if I could do nothing about their concerns, I wanted them to know that the VA in Washington cared.

ception for Vietnam veterans had been so woefully under-done. Consider this revealing and poignant little drama. As part of a continuing effort to help Vietnam vets deal with their feelings of guilt and rejection, a Veterans of Foreign Wars post in the Washington, D.C., area arranged to host about twenty Seattle area veterans for a visit to the memorial wall. During their flight east, the Californians had to change planes in Pittsburgh. Walking through the airport, they saw a huge sign saying WELCOME HOME, GULF VETERANS. It was like a slap in the face, a sharp reminder of what was still missing in their lives. But when they got to Washington the local VFW contingent, including wives and children, was standing at the gate with a sign saying, WELCOME HOME, VIETNAM VETERANS, WE LOVE YOU. The visiting vet-erans wept at the sight. No shame in the tears.

The picture of the fighting man or woman and, conse-quently, the veteran is wildly distorted in much of the cover-age of the Vietnam War. The despairing postwar novels and movies, not to mention virtually live TV footage of combat during the conflict, focus only on horrors. Typical is Oliver Stone's admittedly artistic film *Platoon*. The young soldiers are turned into little more than frightened beasts who freak out on drugs and end up killing each other. One character's concluding line is, "The enemy is us." This sort of message goes down well with people who opposed the war and provides self-justification for those who were "smart" enough or lucky enough to evade it. There is some truth in it, of course. It is saying what General Sherman said more succinctly a hundred years before: "War is hell!" But it is so far removed from the *whole* truth that it has been damaging to millions who survived that hell.

To begin with, *Platoon* lacks historical and political perspective. Whether there should have been one or not, there *was* a very real enemy and it wasn't us. I can testify to that. When they shoot you out of the sky and then torture you to make you give up your faith in your country and betray your comrades, they don't leave you with any doubt about who is the enemy. None of us in uniform were in Vietnam because we wanted to be there or enjoyed the trip. Many, in fact, were drafted. We were all there because our government had decreed that we should be, and our survival depended on outfighting or outwitting that very real enemy. Which brings me to another distortion in that picture. Survival in conditions like those in Vietnam—or in any war, for that matter—depends on a selfless kind of camaraderie—a code of conduct—that can be ennobling. The health-giving memory of war for most veterans is not the hell that they went through but the amazing ability of the human spirit to stand up to it. The strength of that spirit lies in self-sacrificing love, not in hate.

This was the spirit that earned Gen. Norman Schwarzkopf his third Silver Star as a division commander in Vietnam. Legs turned to jelly by honest fear, he crossed a hot mine field to rescue a wounded private when he could have sent a subordinate. There were no parades for Schwarzkopf on his return from Vietnam. Instead, people asked him, "What about the babies you napalmed? What about the villages you burned?" One of the general's homecoming experiences, as related by C.D.B. Bryan in *Reader's Digest*, hit me right where I live. He, his wife and his sister Sally were watching a war movie and he broke out in a sweat when the troops entered a mine field. When his sister asked why he was so affected he tried to tell her what he had gone through and how he felt about it afterward at home. "Well, you have to understand the other side of this thing. Maybe the war protesters were right," Sally said. Schwarzkopf was so upset by the doubts of his own sister that he broke into tears and told her to leave his house. The next day they made up, but the incident is one of the more compelling examples of how the division at home over the Vietnam War impacted the morale of *all* of its participants, including General Schwarzkopf.

Obviously General Schwarzkopf came to grips with Vietnam in his own mind and used it as a stepping-stone to a spectacular career. Indeed, the frustrations that they had faced in Vietnam were factors in the strategy that he and his superior, Gen. Colin Powell, used to achieve a quick, almost bloodless victory in Kuwait. Like these generals, the vast majority of the Vietnam veterans closest to me—my fellow POWs—have led rewarding and productive lives. It would be wrong to say that these lives were not altered and affected by the war. But it would be equally wrong to say that they were ruined. I'm convinced that the rather strange sympathy—or suspicion—about our state of mind and body that I've reported elsewhere in this book is generated by the popular distortions of the veteran's image.

Without calling the whole roll let me cite just a few POWs in evidence for my case. I've already mentioned former Sen. Jeremiah Denton of Alabama and Sen. John McCain of Arizona. Two other POWs have been elected to the House so far—Pete Peterson from northern Florida and Sam Johnson from the Dallas area. Orsen Swindle has been an Assistant Secretary of Commerce; James Warner has been a White House Aide; and Tom Collins is an Assistant Secretary of Labor. Ev Southwick became Deputy Assistant Administrator of NASA. There have been a number of generals and admirals among those who chose a military career. One of these last was my seatmate on the flight out of Hanoi, Bob Shumaker. An electrical engineer like myself, Bob earned his doctorate and became superintendent of the Naval Post Graduate School at Monterey, ending up a rear admiral in charge of half of the Navy's research projects. In "retirement" he has been an assistant dean at George Washington University and associate dean of the Center for Aerospace

Sciences at the University of North Dakota. I have no count of the men who have been successful in private business or those who have been able to put their feet up on the porch railing or to go fishing in quiet contentment.

There's more than anecdotal evidence attesting to the physical and psychological health of a select group of POWs comprised of 168 Navy and Marine pilots who have volunteered to participate in the Repatriated Prisoner of War and Comparison Group Programs at the Naval Aerospace Medical Institute at Pensacola, Florida. I count myself lucky to be in this group. We have been going to Pensacola every year since 1974 to undergo extensive physical and psychological examination. It's the first long-term study of its kind ever made, and it has been under the guidance of Capt. Robert E. Mitchell, MC, USN, since its inception. Throughout, Captain Mitchell has subjected a nonprisoner group to the same battery of tests for comparison purposes. Unfortunately, there hasn't been enough funding or personnel available to make a detailed analysis of the data, but Captain Mitchell was willing to summarize his observations for this book.

"The POWs are doing quite well," he said. "If you look at them in the way of duties performed, for instance, it is obvious. A number of them have been flag officers, commanding officers of major Naval Air Stations. About the same as the control group. But I think that many of the POWs, oddly enough, benefitted by the prison experience. They have been much more aware of what's going on around them. We have often kiddingly said, 'If you want to stay healthy, go to prison for five or six years.'

"A major thing insofar as survival was concerned was the esprit de corps. The group hung together by forming what they called the Fourth Allied Prisoner of War Wing. That helped psychologically. But physically there was not much they could do. With all the torture in the early years they had a lot of damage. Half the study involves psychiatric examination and psychological testing. Out of that whole group I can count on the fingers of one hand the number of individuals who have had psychiatric problems. In some instances, these individuals had problems before their imprisonment. The biggest problems, affecting some 103 individuals, are orthopedic. These come from ejection, hitting the ground, the residuals of torture."

Although he is not a physician, Comdr. Paul E. Galanti, USN (Ret.), has also had an overview of the group as past president of Nam-POWs, Inc., that leads him to conclusions similar to Dr. Mitchell's. "At least ninety percent of them just picked up their lives. The rest turned themselves into self-fulfilling prophecies based on what was said about them in the media and movies," he says. "In fact, my observation is that people who were there over three years were different from the ones captured after. The earlier ones were beat up, tortured, paraded, banged around a lot. I think of them in terms of an ad on TV that shows a blacksmith hammering white hot metal until it turned into a Marine sword."

Admittedly, we POWs had very different backgrounds and experiences than the majority of Vietnam veterans. We were for the most part pilots and officers, and we did not have to slog through the Vietnamese jungles and mine fields or engage in face-to-face combat like the foot soldiers. Instead of being ignored or reviled when we returned, we were sometimes hailed as heroes. So our readjustment to normal life can be challenged as untypical of the Vietnam vet in general. Yet studies show that a vast majority of the rest have coped as well as we have. In the wake of the Vietnam War a new term—Post-Traumatic Stress Disorder (PTSD)—was invented to describe the psychological malaise observable in veterans. This is a serious affliction that can result in alcoholism, divorce, inability to work, drug addiction, violence, depression. A National Vietnam Veterans Readjustment Study completed in 1988 reported: "It is estimated that 15 percent of all male theater veterans are current cases of PTSD. This represents about 470,000 of the estimated 3.4 million men who served in the Vietnam theater. Among females, the prevalence is estimated to be 9 percent of the estimated 7,166 women who served, or about 650 current cases."

Nearly 500,000 individuals constitutes a mass of misery

and maladjustment, but as a percentage of the whole they don't justify the bad image of the Vietnam vet that has pre vailed for so long. One individual with a keen insight into the difference between POWs and the general Vietnam veteran population is Capt. Richard A. Stratton, USN (Ret.). After retirement, Stratton earned a degree at Rhode Island College School of Social Work and is involved with nonprofit counseling of children and Vietnam veterans. He also serves as chairman of the POW Advisory Board for the Department of Veterans Affairs and is a participant in Dr. Mitchell's Pensacola study. Stratton estimates that some 400 out of 4000 Vietnam vets in his Rhode Island county have significant mental health problems, mostly classified as PTSD. Unfortunately, this disorder was neither identified nor counted among veterans of earlier wars, but Stratton says that the same symptoms are surfacing in World War II veterans in this area. Stratton has interesting observations about why the incidence of PTSD is lower among POWs.

"The Navy and Marine Corps were convinced that we would all be nuts," he says. "They told our wives to look out—we'd come home impotent, queer. They were aghast when we came home in a seminormal state. They didn't understand that you're there for six or seven years and after the brutality stops you either sit around and pick mattress stuffing out of your belly button or do something productive. In effect, we ended up doing in prison what I do now with Vietnam vets in group therapy. You sit there and dump out all your doubts and fears with cellmates. Sort out what you have control over and what you don't. Start making plans. We weren't smart enough to know what we were doing but we did it. We took care of our own therapy. Took care of the guilt. We were adjusted to what we had done and hadn't done. We had done our best and tough luck if somebody didn't like it."

Stratton is filling in on what happened in that Fourth Allied Prisoner of War Wing that Dr. Mitchell mentioned. He is also suggesting positive values to be found in a very bad experience. The phrase "comrades in arms" is not the invention of a romantic writer but a reflection of the realities of war. Nor does the camaraderie end with the coming of peace. It is the basis of the large and politically powerful veterans organizations, and it can be seen in purer form in the countless and continuing small reunions of people who served together in a single ship or a company or a division. It is visible on the streets of America during parades on Fourth of July, Memorial Day, Veterans Day. How sharp the contrast between this picture of people who hold each other in respect, even love, and that in a movie like *Platoon*.

The glue in this bonding is not made of the same stuff as that in peacetime friendship—mutual interests, common background, pleasant manners and the like. It's possible, in fact, to dislike a fellow warrior and yet feel bonded to him. The glue is made up of shared fear, mutual trust, loyalty to the same cause, a life-or-death need for each other's support. Warriors also have as long a memory for people who let down the side, people who violated an agreed upon code of conduct, as they do for their trusted comrades. We POWs are no exception. Wonderfully, there were only about a dozen out of more than 500 of us who played along with the North Vietnamese for special privileges such as freedom from torture, better food, early release. Some went so far as to act as assistant jailors. Misjudging the temper of the times at home, we were confident that these turncoats would be severely disciplined by the services and held in disgrace by the American people. But by the time we got home we discovered that we would have to take care of the matter ourselves in the interest of preserving the good name of those who kept the faith.

Officially, Secretary of Defense Melvin R. Laird decreed that alleged offenses by POWs during their time of captivity were to be forgiven. Individual POWs were free to file charges against fellow prisoners on their own, however. The statute of limitations had run out on most of the defectors, but the senior Navy officer among us, Rear Admiral James B. Stockdale, filed charges against Navy Capt. Walter E. Wilber and Marine Col. Edison W. Miller. Both men, he charged, had gained special privileges for providing antiwar, anti-U.S. policy propaganda and had refused to obey orders from senior POW officers. Stockdale's charges included mutiny, aiding the enemy, conspiracy, soliciting other prisoners to violate the Code of Conduct, and causing or attempting to cause insubordination and disloyalty. Although he found merit in the charges, Navy Secretary Warner dismissed them on the grounds that a trial would be disruptive to the lives of too many returnees. He issued letters of censure to Wilbur and Miller and retired them "in the best interests of the naval service."

Not surprisingly, these men haven't been part of the post-war bonding, and for the most part they have stayed out of the public eye. I don't understand how they can even live with themselves, let alone try to pull off Edison Miller's stunt. Turned lawyer, Miller managed to get in with the Jane Fonda/Tom Hayden group in California and was appointed to a vacated seat from Orange County in the state legislature by Gov. Jerry Brown. When his term expired, Miller ran for the office on his own. Word got around the POW circuit, and 168 men signed an ad in the local paper against him. Miller got only twenty percent of the vote, and he filed a libel suit against the men who had signed the ad.

Although I wasn't one of the signers, I agreed to give a deposition on behalf of the defense. I was at the VA then, and a pretty impressive delegation of legal talent arrived from California. There was Miller himself with two attorneys, two more attorneys representing the POWs, a court reporter and a young lady with a video camera. The defense attorneys from one of the largest law firms in California were being paid by USAA, the veterans insurance company that held the automobile and household policies of nearly all 168 defendants. The lawyers for each side sat across from each other at a long conference table in my office. I sat at one end with the court reporter beside me, and the camera woman sat on the other chair. Under direct and cross-examination, I talked for two days from 8:00 A.M. to 4:30 P.M.

I have no love for Miller. Nor he for me, I'm sure. He never even said hello. He sat there stoically silent while I told how he used to carry the keys and lock us up, how he refused to obey the Code of Conduct, how he violated orders of the senior camp officer, how he argued that we were engaged in an evil war. It was the first time that I had spoken so fully about prison experiences. When I had to discuss some of the hard things I would get emotional and choke up. On the second day, the woman attorney on Miller's side started edging away from her client, and the young lady with the video camera came up to me during a break to say that she didn't know much about Vietnam, which was ancient history to her, but that she respected me a lot. During the break I found Miller's male attorney sitting alone, staring up at the ceiling.

"Are you tired." I asked him.

"Oh, no," he said. "It's just that sometimes things don't turn out the way you think they will."

He knew, as I did, that he had no case. When they went in for a pretrial motion a few weeks later, the judge in California threw the whole case out of court.

Blowing the whistle on men like Miller isn't vindictive. It's to alert present and future servicemen and women to the importance of honoring the military Code of Conduct. The people who don't can never know when they might be identified and attacked by another veteran. This happened to Markham Gartley after the outbreak of the Gulf War. He had become something of a public figure in Maine, where he served as secretary of state for Gov. James. B. Longley and ran unsuccessfully for a congressional seat. Knowing that he had been a Navy pilot and a four-year POW in Vietnam, the Associated Press interviewed Gartley about the new war. In establishing his authority to speak about matters military, the article did not mention that Gartley had been released early by our captors to return home with his mother who had come to Hanoi on a peace mission. But a veteran with a sharp eye and long memory saw the story and boiled over.

In an article printed in the Bangor *Daily News*, Lt. Col. James M. Sexton of the Maine Air National Guard, who had flown 238 combat missions in Vietnam, wrote:

"Gartley's less than honorable acceptance of amnesty from his captors makes him an inappropriate spokesman. When Gartley and two other POWs were released into the hand of anti-war protesters, which included Gartley's mother, it made headlines. Many in the military were incredulous that they would accept parole in direct violation of the Code of Conduct. To understand my concern, it's necessary to understand the concepts of the Code of Conduct. Article III of the code states, 'If I am captured I will continue to resist by all means available. I will make every effort to escape and aid others to escape. I will accept neither parole nor special favors from the enemy.' A POW is legally bound by the Uniform Code of Military Justice and ethically guided by the Code of Conduct."

One of Gartley's statements about the Gulf War was that "all wars are wrong," judging by moral standards. Perhaps he reached that conclusion in Vietnam. The rest of us didn't. Having had communist thinking shoved down our throats by torture and having seen the misery of the people held in its thrall, we appreciated our government's *good intentions* in trying to help the South Vietnamese fend it off. I think that Ronald Reagan said it right: it was a noble venture. Two things went wrong. Politically, the governing elements in South Vietnam were weak. Militarily, the war was fought from Washington rather than in the field. Until there is an ideal world there are bound to be less than ideal wars in which young American men and women will have to fight. The worse the war from a political point of view, the more the warriors will need at least the understanding of their fellow citizens.

As the debate in the churches and Congress about the Gulf War showed, the wisest, most sincere people can disagree strongly about the morality of war. Quite apart from the disputed issue of justification, war continually confronts its participants with difficult moral dilemmas. Still the most agonizing of these was the decision that the Commander-in-Chief, Harry Truman, had to face when he learned that the United States had a workable atomic bomb. In a similar situation on a smaller scale during the Vietnam War, my friend Admiral Bud Zumwalt made the same choice with tragic consequences. He ordered defoliation with Agent Orange to be stepped up in the area where his son, Elmo, was

At the dedication of the Vietnam Veterans statue in Washington in 1984, I had a solemn talk with the man who symbolized the American military effort there, General William Westmoreland.

commanding a fast boat. After the war, Elmo developed cancer and his son, Russell, the admiral's grandson, suffered birth defects. The Zumwalts were convinced that these ailments were caused by Elmo's exposure to the Agent Orange despite the fact that there was no sure scientific proof. Neither man knew that Agent Orange might have such side effects while they were in Vietnam. Yet, in light of the tragedy, both men say that they would have performed in the same manner even if they had known of the possible consequences. Their sense of the right moral choice for dedicated military personnel is made clear by two brief statements from the book they wrote jointly, *My Father, My Son*:

ELMO: "I do not second-guess the decisions Dad made in Vietnam, nor do I doubt for a minute that the saving of human life was always his first priority in his conduct of the war. I have the greatest love and admiration for him as

Nothing made me happier during my years of VA service than marching with Vietnam veterans who were gradually regaining their pride, as on this occasion in New York City in 1985.

a man, and the deepest respect for him as a military leader. Certainly thousands, including me, are alive today because of his decision to use Agent Orange. I do not hold him responsible for what happened to Russell and me. And knowing what I know now, and facing what I now face, I cannot say I am sorry, or feel any bitterness, for volunteering to go to Vietnam. I made the choice and created my own destiny.''

ADMIRAL ZUMWALT: ''Because of the orders I gave ... I was responsible for Elmo's heavy exposure to Agent Orange, which makes me an instrument in his tragedy. Elmo and I know each other so well that I never thought he would hold me responsible, nor did he think I would feel guilty. Had I not used Agent Orange, many more lives would have been lost in combat, perhaps even Elmo's. And knowing what I now know, I still would have ordered the defoliation to achieve the objectives it did. But that does not ease the sorrow I feel for Elmo, or the anguish his illness, and Russell's disability, give me. It is the first thing I think of when I awake in the morning, and the last thing I remember when I go to sleep at night."

Unfortunately for those who like to view life in black and white instead of shades of gray, scientific studies since the Zumwalt book was written, including those that Harry Walters and I initiated at the Center for Disease Control, have not identified Agent Orange as the villain in this sort of drama. But, with veterans affairs being as highly politicized as I've noted, both Congress and VA Secretary Edward J. Derwinski have done so on their own by authorizing disability payments to veterans with the skin disease chloracne and two forms of cancer—soft-tissue sarcoma and non-Hodgkin's lymphoma. Essentially, it's an extension of the position Harry and I took when we offered medical treatment to anyone who claimed to be a victim of Agent Orange. At the heart of the matter is Lincoln's charge to care for veterans in distress regardless of the specific cause. And I believe that Lincoln, who met personally with many soldiers and their families, made this charge because he detected in them the attitude of service above self that the Zumwalts display.

Whether the Veterans Administration, now the Department of Veterans Affairs, is the best instrument for the nation to use in discharging its obligation to the men and women who have served it in war is a moot question. I have not been able to detect any serious opposition to either its existence or its general program. On the contrary, one element in Robert Nimmo's demise as administrator was that he used the word "mainstream," which is anathema to the powerful veterans organizations. That word covers a concept of giving veterans vouchers to use facilities in the mainstream of medical care rather than creating facilities especially for them. What people often forget is that the VA system has ancillary benefits for society. Most of the problems it solves for the veterans are not service-connected, and it cares for the aged and the indigent. To do away with it would mean dumping a new load on the general hospitals and the nation's welfare system. Aside from providing care, the VA institutions perform vital educational and research functions for the whole medical establishment, especially the teaching medical schools.

Unless and until the nation no longer has a significant number of veterans among the population, the present system is here to stay. But the administration, Congress, and the public should be looking for right answers to some questions. Is the VA system being run as efficiently as possible? What share of the national wealth can be—should be—devoted to the care of veterans? Could VA services be better integrated with *some* areas of "mainstream" services, public and private? Are there more self-help measures like the GI educational program that could be developed to reduce handouts? The whole subject of veteran care is deserving of more hard thought and less political posturing than it gets.

I am a special pleader when I argue that veterans deserve the best. But I don't think that the best is synonymous with the most, since we veterans are citizens and taxpayers, too. My hope is that the new appreciation of America's military people generated by the Gulf War will result in an equally new resolve to deal intelligently and sympathetically with their problems *after* the shooting stops.

CHAPTER XII

Tough Times

In JANUARY, 1986, Harry Walters announced that he was going to resign from the Veterans Administration to return to private business. He asked me if I would be interested in stepping into his shoes. People in the White House were sending out feelers in my direction, he told me. This caused me do some hard soul-searching. It represented more of an honor than before since the machinery was grinding away to upgrade the position to cabinet-level Secretary of Veterans Affairs. It also represented an opportunity to continue doing worthwhile work that I enjoyed and could perform well. But what would happen in two years? Everybody in the administration was sure that a Republican—most likely George Bush—would be elected and that I would be asked to continue in service. But could I count on that? Not in the light of one lesson that a life like mine had drummed into my skull: there are no guarantees.

Realistically, I would have to face the possibility of being on the street in two years. I wasn't getting any younger, and my children were getting older. We had put the boys in a private Catholic school. High school, with tuition bills that would be onerous, was yet to come and, when they reached college age the bills would be staggering. Having been in government service continually since I left college, I hadn't accumulated a nest egg or secured a position in the private sector, like most of my colleagues, as political appointees. I'd had to forego my Navy retirement pay since joining the Peace Corps. No question we were living well compared to the standards of my childhood, but I felt that I owed it to my family's future to consider finding some more stable kind of employment in the private sector.

I'd long since decided that at forty-eight I was too old and had too many responsibilities to begin to establish myself in the legal profession. The rewards were there, but they quite rightly went to the people who were willing and able to accumulate clients over a period of time or work their way up

Whatever I managed to do for veterans was returned to me tenfold. In just one instance of gratitude, I was given the Veterans of Foreign Wars Gold Citizenship Award in Dallas, Texas, in 1985. My family came along, and we made a short vacation of the trip.

My work was appreciated "at the office," as well. Handing me a certificate to that effect is VA Administrator Harry Walters. With different but complementary personalities, we made a good team, and I chose to leave when he did in January, 1986.

inside a firm. In the health field the VA's outreach is considerable, and it wasn't long before I had a good offer from there. In May, 1986, I resigned as the VA's deputy administrator to become Vice-President, Government Operations, of the Hospital Corporation of America.

Although the new job was promising, challenging and financially rewarding, the parting wasn't easy for me. I was fond of my colleagues at the VA and still genuinely concerned about its clientele—the veterans. I'd had my problems with the White House as an organization but none with its chief residents. In view of the help that she had given me along the way, I felt obliged to explain my decision personally to Nancy Reagan. She invited me to her private quarters at the White House. She was not happy with my news. I guess she had a feeling that the rats were jumping ship as the administration wound down. When I went into my financial needs she said,

"Well, I guess we'd all like to be millionaires." I went home very disappointed. But a few days later there came a letter on stationery headed "The White House, Washington" that read:

May 10, 1986

Dear Ev:

It is with deep personal regret that I accept your resignation as Deputy Administrator of Veterans' Affairs. Your 26-year career of service to this Nation has been marked with valor, dedication and a keen sense of caring. As a naval officer shot down over North Vietnam and held prisoner for eight and one-half years, you displayed courage and determination that serves as a model for all Americans to emulate.

After leaving the Naval service you assumed a new role as a key member of another vital organization, the Peace Corps. You brought to government an understanding of the importance of helping others. That attitude is one which you have used since your arrival at the VA nearly four years ago to advance the quality of care and concern given to this country's 28 million veterans.

As President and Commander in Chief, I want you to know that this Nation appreciates the support and dedication you have given to serving our veterans. Your efforts are obvious to me, but more importantly they are manifested in a growing national pride in our veterans and what they stand for and stood for. Morale is high among VA employees and that translates into improved services for veterans. And finally, your personal involvement in modernizing and improving fiscal and management programs has made the Veterans' Administration a solid and vital part of this Administration's dream.

Ev, as you and Tammy go forward in your new endeavors, know that Nancy and I wish you fair winds and a following sea.

Sincerely,
Ronald Reagan

That letter made me feel much better as I set up shop in the HCA offices on the tenth floor of one of the high rises in Rosslyn, a section of Arlington, Virginia, across the Potomac River from Washington. From my window I had a panoramic view with a sweep from Georgetown down through the memorial mall with the Capitol rising behind to the fringe of the National Airport. Although corporate headquarters were in Nashville we were stationed in the Washington area to try to sell HCA's services to the federal government. We were particularly interested in becoming part of the military's Comprehensive Health and Medical Programs for the United States (CHAMPUS), an experiment in the care of active duty dependents and retirees by contracting out for services. With HCA's national chain of hospitals we seemed to be in a good position to propose a major hospital-care network to the government. For six months or so after I started on the job, things went well. Then suddenly I fell into a real-life Catch-22.

Early in 1987 rumors floated through the company that HCA would divest itself of its hospitals that were losing money. If that were to happen we wouldn't have the package that we were trying to sell the CHAMPUS. On the other hand, our operation had been launched to counteract the hard times in the health-care industry that were causing the hospitals to lose money. What Nashville hadn't taken into account was the time and patience required to do business with the government. In the face of mounting losses and a threat of a leveraged buyout, HCA management started thrashing around in all directions to improve the corporation's financial position. The government negotiations were shifted to a group called Equicorp, combining HCA, Equitable Life and Blue Cross/Blue Shield of South Carolina, and then dropped altogether. By July we were told that our division would be phased out entirely. There was nothing left to do but try to negotiate the best possible separation terms.

The news that I would be out of a job hit me at a particularly awkward time. My hometown had asked me to be the Grand Marshal for the annual Salinas, California, rodeo and to take part in a reunion in recognition of naming a new high school after me. My family had busy plans of their own for the time I would be gone. Marc, just turned thirteen, was away from home for the first time at a summer camp in the mountains near Ligonier, Pennsylvania. Being protective parents, we had checked thoroughly and felt that Marc was in good hands at a camp run by the East Liberty Presbyterian Church in Pittsburgh. While I was in California Tammy and Bryan would drive up from Washington, pick up Marc and a Washington friend, Steve Mahoney, whose parents were away, and spend a few days with my mother-in-law in Munhall, outside of Pittsburgh. With all this going on, worry about a job was not what we needed.

A phone call made everything else pale by comparison. It was the camp director on the phone from a hospital near Latrobe, a town close to Ligonier. There had been an accident, and they needed approval for Marc to go into immediate surgery for damage to his legs. Eruptive as she can be, Tammy turned into a cool-headed doctor's daughter during the next crucial moments. She asked questions about the surgeon and learned that he was expert in orthopedics. She talked to Marc, already heavily sedated, on the phone. She was somewhat reassured by the nonchalant tone of his voice and the fact that he was praying. Before giving her blessing, though, she called Washington and got confirmation of the surgeon's reputation from her brother-in-law. Then she called a cousin to drive her to Latrobe, threw some clothes into a suitcase and started out into the night in the hope of getting to Marc before the operation.

Tammy's true state was graphically described by ten-year-old Bryan, a fascinated observer of the scene in a household consisting of three emotional women—his mother, grandmother, and great-aunt. "Mom says she wasn't excited," Bryan recalls, "but she left without her underwear and had to come back because she had no underwear under her clothes." The ride did little to calm her. When she learned the details of the accident at the hospital, she threw her overnight case at the camp director for allowing this to happen to her son. What with the time changes and the trouble in reaching me in California—I'd taken off for a few days to try to sort out my life—Tammy decided to bear all this anxiety herself until she could tell me more about Marc's condition and what had to be done for him.

Her throwing the overnight case seems altogether justified by the facts of the situation. That Wednesday the program at camp was white-water rafting on a mountain river. The thirty-nine campers were rousted out of bed at 5:00 A.M. by four counselors and taken by bus and van about ninety miles to the river, where they had an exciting but exhausting day. With thirty kids in the bus and thirteen in the van, they started back to camp. About 7:00 P.M. they were driving along Route 711 just off the Pennsylvania Turnpike when the weary counselor at the wheel of a van full of dozing kids apparently fell asleep himself. The van left the road and went careening down a steep incline through a tangle of trees to a creek bottom a hundred or more feet below. By some miracle the van didn't smash directly into a tree or roll over. But the van had side doors that kept opening and shutting as it scraped against trees. Marc, who had been sitting on a wheel well in back, was flung around so that his lower legs got caught between the slamming door and the body of the van. When the van came to rest at the bottom, a few kids were able to scramble out, but Marc and some others with broken legs could not. Miraculously, nobody was killed.

Rescuers had to get the injured out of the gully with ropes on stretchers and rush them to the hospital in Latrobe. Those with head injuries were triaged and sent to Pittsburgh. But with an experienced orthopedist on hand in the emergency room it was decided to give Marc and others with broken bones preliminary treatment in Latrobe. In Marc's case it was very preliminary. There were compound fractures in both legs, and a large piece of flesh was missing on his right leg; the ankle part of his left foot was shattered. All they could do in those six hours at Latrobe was to clean the wounds without causing further damage. Since surgical reconstruction of the feet and ankles would take such a long time and so many operations, Tammy, in consultation with the local doctors and her brother-in-law in Washington, decided to take

Marc and his friend Steve, who had a broken leg, back home.

Once this was decided Tammy tried to reach me on Thursday from Latrobe, where she was staying with Marc. Knowing that I might check in with my office, she called Ted Wood, another HCA vice-president in Washington, and my sister Delia in San Jose and asked them to contact me. They both tried, but didn't get to me until Friday morning (afternoon in the East) when I called my office. "Oh, thank God, it's you!" my secretary said, and switched me right to Ted Wood. He broke the news gently. "Marc's been in an accident, Ev, but he'll be OK. You'd better call Tammy. Here's her number in Latrobe." Holding back on details, Tammy said that, yes, Marc had broken his legs but was in good spirits. There was no point in my trying to get to Latrobe, she told me, since they would be moving him to Washington. The best thing I could do was to keep in touch.

Next to being shot down I went through the worst time of my life. Once again I felt helpless. I could do nothing but pray for the son whose birth had restored me to a full, feeling life. *Why him, Lord, and not me*? Tammy's instructions made all kinds of sense, but they left me terribly frustrated.

After talking again to Tammy that afternoon I drove to my mother's home in Santa Clara, where we could stay in constant touch. Plans were firmed up in Latrobe for an ambulance to carry Marc and Steve to our home in Rockville on Sunday with Tammy, her mother and Bryan following in our car. Tammy's brother-in-law had arranged for Marc and Steve to be seen on Monday by Dr. Rick Reff, one of Washington's top orthopedists. I wanted to meet them in Washington but Tammy argued that there was nothing I could do that wasn't already being done, that she had plenty of help from her family and that I had important and long-standing obligations to the people in Salinas who were counting on me for that rodeo on Sunday and the school ceremonies on Monday. I could attend to these and still be home before Marc had to undergo any further procedures, she insisted. I unhappily accepted Tammy's logic and went robotlike through the two-day program.

Dr. Reff sent Steve back to recuperate at Rockville, where Tammy had turned the family room into a makeshift hospital ward until his parents could return from Europe. He ordered Marc into Children's Hospital to be prepared for surgery. Enlisting the help of Dr. John Gronvall, then medical director of the VA, Tammy arranged to stay with Marc in a room at the hospital while her mother looked after Steve at home. Word of the accident spread through the VA hospital that sits right next to Children's Hospital, and a stream of VA people came over to check on Marc and see what they could do for Tammy. Dr. Gronvall and his wife Cindy got up on Wednesday morning in time to meet the "Red Eye" flight from San Francisco, landing at Dulles Airport at 6:00 A.M., and rush me to the hospital. To try to lighten the mood for Marc I was wearing the boots and cowboy hat that had been my outfit for the rodeo parade. Tammy was down in the cafeteria having breakfast, and Marc was alone when I walked into his room. He was lying there with casts up to the hips on both legs. But as full of vinegar as his mother, Marc greeted his "comic" cowboy old man with a smile. I took my son in my arms. What a relief to hold and hug him and feel how *alive* he was!

Within an hour of my arrival they wheeled Marc off for another six hours of surgery—the first of three operations to rebuild the bone structure and perform plastic surgery on the left foot and ankle. I sent Tammy home and settled down to live with Marc in the hospital. Confirmation of our termination came from HCA. So, I would go to the office during the day, and it was during Marc's two-week hospital stay that the details were worked out. The separation agreement was good considering the short time of my employment. To Ted Wood and me and all of us in Washington, the company's CEO Tommy Frist, Jr., it was apologetic: "You guys are gentlemen and you've been very honest with us and hard working and I appreciate it. I'm sorry to do what I have to do."

Apologies and good will don't put bread on the table. I had to do something soon—but what? My first venture into the supposedly rich land of corporate America was ending in disaster. Sure, I could find another job with another company, but couldn't the same thing happen again? I remembered my father's seesaw life with strikes and layoffs and other events beyond his control. I remembered my father-in-law's advice to become independent. I decided that if anybody was ever again going to kill me off, at least in the sense of losing a job, it would be me, not "them." At hand was a form of self-employment I was very familiar with from my service in government. There are probably as many consultants as there are lawyers and lobbyists in Washington. The reason is that outsiders seeking to do business in the maze of the Washington wonderland are truly in need of an expert guide. With my background I felt I could qualify as such a guide. Anyway, it was worth a try.

Through my "network" I got a client—Acer Technologies, a Taiwan-based company that was selling its computers in the United States. They would pay a fee for my help in dealing with the government as a potential customer. It was enough to enable me to rent a small office about a block from the White House and set about looking for more clients. At the same time Nick Onorato, my right-hand man at both the Peace Corps and the VA, and I began having talks about starting a consulting business that would be broader and more versatile than what either of us could do alone. During that fall of 1987 we recruited Kevin Riley as a third partner and vice-president and decided to go ahead in the new year. In terms of challenge and promise it was an exciting prospect, but we all knew that there would be no money in sight for who knew how long.

Which meant there would be belt-tightening in Rockville far more severe than in the days of my law-clerking. We had to dig deep into savings, sell a lot we had acquired for a sometime vacation home in Idaho, get rid of my beloved 1976 BMW. In short, get real. Tammy got a part-time teaching job. We pulled together as a family to answer Tammy's repeated call to arms: "Dad has to start a new business, and Marc has to get well!"

Marc's was the worst deal of our tough times. From July until Thanksgiving he was immobilized in those casts and often in pain. Nothing I went through in Vietnam was harder for me to bear than to see the suffering of my son. We had him bedded down in the family room, and for all of that time I slept on a couch beside him. I wanted to be there if he ever woke up with a nightmare, and somebody had to be on hand to help him urinate or move his bowels. For a boy so young boredom and frustration were as hard to take as pain. Good and game for the most part, he would sometimes rebel against his fate and take it out on us. Once he refused to eat, and one of our POW friends living in the Washington area, Charlie Zuhoski, came to our rescue. My boys have always been able to take things from Charlie that they wouldn't take from me, and I think I've had the same effect on his kids. On this occasion Charlie just talked turkey to Marc about how he was hurting himself and hurting us, and turned the boy around.

Even when Marc was able to get up and go back to school, the future of the Alvarez enterprise as a whole remained in real doubt. But I'm a natural optimist, the kind of guy who sees the glass half-full. I can't ever remember consciously acquiring this attitude. I do know that it was part of my survival equipment in Hanoi, and I also know that it can sometimes drive people around me crazy. There was the time, for instance, when Tammy was fretting about going to the dentist for a tooth extraction. "Don't think about the worst," I told her. "Just think that it will be over soon." "Oh, stop it," she said, "I just want you to be miserable with me." I was properly told off.

For all the years of our marriage, though, Tammy's faith in the future—and in me—has been rock solid, a sure foundation for the whole family. Through most of 1987 and 1988 we were down, but with optimism and faith on our side we never conceded that we might be out.

CHAPTER XIII

Speaking Out

WHILE I WAS GOING through a time of troubles professionally and within the family I was also entering into a new and fulfilling phase of my life. I was learning to talk about my Vietnam experience. When the occasion arose I had of course confided in Tammy about some of the events of prison days and my feelings about them. Once in a long while I had opened up a bit to a sympathetic military audience such as fellow naval officers at Lemoore Naval Air Station. But for the most part I had kept the memories of that struggle for survival buttoned up inside, as if hoping that they would go away. I hadn't even shared them with my family in California or my closest colleagues at work. My top aide at the Veterans Administration, Leo Wurschmidt, recently recalled, "Ev never brought one POW story to the VA. I worked with him three and a half years and we talked about his experience maybe once or twice. He was professional at all times."

Whether I was being professional or simply overindulging in that emotional suppression—"stuffing it down," a psychologist once called it—that served me so well in captivity remains a good question. But, whether I liked it or not, I was in constant contact with bad results of this suppression through my efforts to help Vietnam veterans at the VA. It was both moving and enlightening to witness the evident healing when men at the Vietnam memorial wall finally released their anger, pain, guilt, sorrow. The audiences I confronted when I went around the country to make speeches as part of my job gave me pause to think. I tried to stick to general veterans' issues, but they kept pumping me through their questions for personal stories and comment about surviving as a POW. They wanted to know how not only I but the rest of the men had done it. The general interest in the subject was reflected in sales of books by other POWs and in attendance at their speeches. Jerry Coffee, for instance, had made spreading the message we talked about in the Hanoi Hilton his duty at the end of his naval service and a full-time career in retirement.

A turning point for me came when I was contacted in 1985 by Philip Straw, a staff member for Representative Clarence Miller of Ohio, who moonlights as a professor at the University of Maryland. Straw was a Vietnam veteran himself, decorated for valor in combat as a Marine officer. He conceived and sold to the university the idea for a course called Honors 318, "America in Vietnam," dealing with all aspects of that war. It quickly became one of the most popular courses on campus. Straw wanted to know if I would join Air Force Col. Fred Cherry, the first black pilot POW, as a guest for one of his classes. I agreed since I have never been able to resist an opportunity to be with young people, and I was amazed by their intense interest in events that occurred before many of them were born.

Confronted by these eager students, I couldn't hold back. They wanted to know how it actually was, all the grisly details. I found myself telling them about the worms—how the first time I saw a worm in my stool I screamed for the guard. He told me that everyone in North Vietnam had worms. "It's good," he said. "If you don't have worms, your stomach bloats." Eventually we POWs had contests to see who could pass the longest worm, and I scored with a twelve-incher. Even as I was recounting this I realized that I was illustrating the value of humor in accepting and enduring bad situations. Like Jerry Coffee's, the message I had to spread was more positive than negative.

As a member of Captain Mitchell's group in Pensacola I shared the emerging consensus that keeping honor intact throughout the POW experience had actually strengthened us in spite of some lingering physical pain and disability. It would be hard not to gain strength from incidents like the one involving Navy Lt. (jg.) Ed Davis who occupied a cell next to mine for a while. The North Vietnamese were torturing him. He was tied up, and every hour on the hour they would come in and beat him. When I was sure that they were gone I would communicate with him through the wall in our tap code to let him know that he wasn't alone. Once when there had been nothing but silence from his cell for hours I was afraid that he had died. "Are you OK? Are you in pain?" I tapped. He lightly tapped back, "What's life without a little pain?"

No doubt we all view the strengthening process in slightly different terms, but we all agree that it was effective. Listen to a few POW voices:

PAUL GALANTI: "Why do the POWs have such a good success record in later life? We got pushed way beyond anything we thought we could take for a very long time. Everybody had time to reassess values. Most of us were in solitary for extended periods, which makes you think a little deeper than your average fighter pilot tends to. We were forced into evaluating ourselves and making some resolutions."

CHARLIE ZUHOSKI: "The thing that prison did for me and probably for a lot of others was to give me a willingness to try things. I think the experience in prison removed our inhibitions to a certain extent. To be locked in and confined and prevented from anything for so long a period of time makes you realize that life is too short to allow your inhibitions to prevent you from anything. So you try. The other thing about prison is that you put the past behind you. The worst words in the vocabulary are *should have, could have*.

If you made a mess of things, your objective is to clean up the mess, not to figure out what you could have done to avoid the mess."

BOB SCHUMAKER: "It's a tough school to go through, but in a perverse sense I think I am a better person as a result of the experience. I was an engineer and sometimes engineers get a little myopic in thinking that the world is made up of pure science. All of us learned over there that there is a human side of things—feelings to consider and motivation factors. It was an area lacking in my life that got filled."

KEN CORDIER: "The greatest thing we took away from there has to do with personal relationships, getting a better appreciation for the other guy's point of view. I think I'm more considerate than I used to be. Living in that pressure environment for as long as we did was sort of like a graduate degree in human relations. When you are locked up twenty-four hours a day with the same guys for a year and a half, having no privacy in 18 by 24 feet with a couple of rusty bricks for a toilet, you learn to get along with people. It made me more effective than I would have been otherwise. It also made me more goal oriented than I would have been—to try to make the best use of the time I've got on this planet. I always say I adjusted to prison about two years into the experience when I was sitting there on my board and I said to myself, 'This is your life.' That's when I got serious about learning language skills and the like, about making the best of it."

DICK STRATTON: "It was a good weight-reduction program but I couldn't recommend it. Seriously, it was a growing experience. A lot of people didn't like the way they were going and turned it around. Common denominators in those who survived? Sense of humor. Pretty good family, neighborhood, church and school background. Basically our roots. It meant that anybody who had those good formative years could survive the situation."

FRED CHERRY: "I was what I was when I went there, but I became more aware of what I was. I also became more aware of not bringing harm to anyone else."

By 1986 I was ready when Anthony S. Pitch, a writer living in nearby Potomac, Maryland, approached me with a proposal that we collaborate on a book about those lost years, the years of captivity. There were many reasons why the timing was right. Having quit the government, I was free to speak out. Having completed my education, I had time to spare and was in need of whatever extra income the book might bring. A happy second marriage and family life had long since healed the hurt of my first wife's desertion. I sensed that the public was at last ready for the kind of book I wanted to produce instead of another anguished look at the humiliation and divisiveness of the Vietnam War. Publisher Donald I. Fine agreed, and over the course of the next three years Pitch and I created *Chained Eagle*.

The very process of writing the book became a catharsis for the Alvarez family. For me, it was like uncorking a bottle of fizzing soda. The more I got into it, the more intense I became. The more I talked about it, the more I wanted to talk. I hadn't wanted to talk about my first wife, for instance. In thirteen years, I had never visited her, but when she became an integral part of my story I was able to see her in perspective. The thoughts and feelings that I hadn't been able to share with my parents and sisters came bubbling out. From the tapes they made for my collaborator, I heard for the first time details of what they had endured on my behalf. As I suspected, Delia's motive for getting involved in antiwar activities was to do something—anything—to promote my release. But her involvement led to an intellectual and moral conviction about the war's evil every bit as strong as my counterview. My mother went along with Delia, and it exacerbated the already serious difficulties with my father, who thought that the way to help was to keep quiet. My notoriety made their lives a torment of reporters invading their privacy. We are all strong personalities. Learning about each other's ordeals has not led to agreement, but it has brought about a healing that allows us to communicate more openly with each other.

The kind of conversations we can have now are reflected in

an exchange between Delia and me when she was visiting us in Maryland during the Gulf War:

EVERETT: "This peace movement this time is a regular commercial off-the-shelf movement. One day we had a hundred thousand people out there. Right off the shelf."

DELIA: "Well, it's a cross section. Do you know where the peace vigils were before the war started? In suburbia, in the churches—people from all walks of life."

EVERETT: "Do you know the difference between these peace marchers right now and Vietnam? They say they oppose the war but they support the warriors. In Vietnam the image of the veteran was hurt. At the VA I saw the damage done. Who put this negative image on them? Why? That's what really bothered me. It's a few people who are very influential. Oliver Stone, for instance. You can have *Born on the Fourth of July*. He had a problem with the whole thing. He thrives on this negative thing."

DELIA: "I saw those movies depicting the vet being victim, and I think that it really helped the healing process."

EVERETT: "Being victimized? I had a person tell me, 'You were victimized.' In that context anybody who ever fought in a war was victimized."

DELIA: "I think the movies Oliver Stone has done really helped middle America see what the vets went through."

EVERETT: "Let me tell you what I think Oliver Stone did. He combined the negatives and left out the positives. Do you know who opposed his depiction of the Vietnam vet? The Vietnam vets themselves. They said, 'Yeah, what he did was he took bad segments, things that happened, and did a good job in producing it. But they did a lot of good. What good did the Vietnam vet do if you saw Oliver Stone?' "

DELIA: "He raised the consciousness—"

EVERETT: "But he left the wrong impression."

Agreement? No. Communication? Yes. On that same night we got into the Chicano movement, too. It had proved divisive throughout the whole Alvarez/Sanchez family. Delia, an activist herself, told how she had tried to defend me with her activist friends and relatives who were disappointed when I didn't carry the Chicano banner. In her words: "I said, 'Hey, wait a minute! Everett's been in prison. He's been alone for a long while. My brother, he's conservative. You've got brothers who are conservatives, too.' " For my part I told her how I had resisted being a Mexican-American token in government. We did agree that we had both escaped the Mexican stereotype and gone farther than most of the kids we grew up with because of our parents' insistence on achievement and the examples they set. As Delia put it: "We had obstacles to overcome to become achievers. But it was an achieving ambience that we grew up in. I think both parents were over-achievers. But they never had the opportunities."

Although I have often taken a stand against ethnic divisiveness, I appreciate my Mexican roots and cherish acknowledgements from my compatriots that I represent them well. Here, World War II Mexican veterans representing Air Squadron 201 presented me with a trophy.

Leaving government has not ended my role as a spokesman, especially with respect to veterans' or Mexican-American affairs. In 1989, I spoke at the Department of Labor during National Hispanic Heritage Month.

With the publication of my book and the attendant publicity, I got invitations to speak to all kinds of audiences all over the country. Struggling to get on my feet financially, I was in no position to respond to these invitations without reimbursement of expenses and some sort of fee. I have a hard time asking for remuneration and a harder time saying no, especially when veterans or schools are involved. Early on I had an embarrassing but educational experience that led me to seek professional help. I was asked to speak in Kentucky on a Veterans Day. I brought up the subject of an honorarium and the woman on the phone, a secretary in the governor's office, mentioned $500. I went. I spoke and I returned without getting any money. Then there arrived in the mail a personal check for $500 from the secretary. I called her for an explanation. "Well," she said, "I personally wanted you to come and there weren't any state funds for the purpose and so ..." I sent back the check and went to see Gloria Gilbert, a partner in Speakers Unlimited, Inc., who has represented me ever since.

Jerry Coffee claims that an honest man has only one speech. He's right in terms of testimony about personal experience, which, after all, is the foundation of the speeches we give. But I quickly learned how to tailor the testimony to the interests of the audience while keeping the essential shape of the message. To make a pattern for the tailoring I have to do, I usually ask my hosts why they invited me. Len Malkin, a vice-president of New York's Manufacturers Hanover Trust, hoped that hearing from a survivor about the kind of problems we had in prison would make a conference of branch managers think that their seemingly insoluble problems were maybe not so tough after all. Nat Daniels, Dean of Liberal Arts at rural Rio Grande College in Ohio, wanted me for a course that he privately calls "Anti-Provincialism 101," a look at what is going on in the world beyond the students' limited horizon. There I was a living witness to what the Vietnam War was all about and the sacrifices it exacted from American citizens. Down at the very tip of Texas, at Texas University Pan American in Edinburg, where eighty-six percent of the 12,000 students are Mexican-Americans, Sandy Rodriguez, Coordinator of Student Activities, sought me out as a role model of what a person with an ethnic and economic background similar to that of those students could achieve.

It probably isn't hard to see how I cut the cloth of the story I've been relating in this book for each of those audiences. Here, however, I want to deal in the basic material of that cloth and let the reader make use of it as he or she can. Like the threads that are interwoven to create a strong piece of material, each theme is an essential strand in the message that I want to get across. Basically, it's that the beliefs and attitudes necessary for survival with honor during the worst conditions of war or disaster are useful in so-called normal life and vice-versa. I've tried to illustrate this with that indispensable lubricant of the spirit called humor. Here are some other character traits of survivors as I've known them.

A CODE OF CONDUCT. There are rules for every game, laws for every civilization. Without them there would be chaos. In our case, as POWs, these were spelled out in an established Code of Conduct that begins this book. Under extreme duress we discovered that it was humanly impossible to survive and still adhere to the letter of this code. But it was possible to adhere to its spirit. By forcing our captors to torture us into submission every time, we often made them weary of the effort, and we certainly convinced them that we were not on their side or converted to their thinking. We never went into an interrogation or torture session not knowing what we ought to do.

In the end, the unbreakable rule—the code as amended in the Hanoi Hilton—was: *Do your best.* The way I put it to myself was: "Someday I'm going to walk out of here, and when I do I'll want to look myself in the mirror and face my family and my friends without being ashamed." This is something anybody can say to himself or herself every day. But there's no way of knowing whether you are doing your best unless you have a code that you can't quite live up to.

There are many such codes that human beings have found sound and inspiring. I tell young people that the Boy Scout Oath is a civilian equivalent of the Code of Conduct. And there are the Ten Commandments, the Sermon on the Mount. As an athlete I would even consider "being a good sport" an adequate code if observed in all its connotations.

A BELIEF IN SOMETHING GREATER THAN SELF. It's one thing to have a code and quite another to summon up the guts to stick to it under duress. Self-preservation is the strongest natural human drive. What is commonly called courage is the willingness to risk self-destruction in obedience to some authority or in pursuit of some purpose that a person decides is more important than self. Good soldiers (not to mention policemen, firemen, lifesavers and the like) do this routinely.

Under most circumstances the source of this courage is the person's own physical and psychological armament. As a fighter pilot, for instance, I took off on combat missions without debilitating fear because I was confident that the skill I had acquired in training and the plane I was flying would pull me through. Had they done so, I might be spreading a message of pure self-reliance today.

I can say quite honestly that I was scared right down to the socks when my plane started falling out of the sky. Like most human beings, I was afraid of dying, and I had lost all control over whether I would live or die. I have since heard the postcrash cockpit recorders of civilian pilots in the same situation. Often—and I'm not passing judgment—the last words from some pilots are "oh, shit!"—words of disgusted resignation. If I had hit land instead of water, with a recorder going, my last words would have been "Our Father which art in heaven . . ." They simply gushed out of me, rose like an oil strike from a well filled by all those years as a believing altar boy and student at Santa Clara. An attitude of resignation might be adequate in that mysterious realm beyond death, but I can testify that it won't work when you have to go on living for years in a perpetual state of having all control of your life in hostile hands.

That instinctive act of prayer later became a conscious act, my mainstay in the early months of imprisonment when I was all alone and completely at my captors' mercy. As I've said, I carved a crude altar in the cell wall, resurrected the words of Mass from memory. At first I thought that I would devote an hour to worship. That turned out to be an hour that was *gone*. I looked forward to it. So I started doing it morning and evening. It took my mind away from what was there and it gave me something else to think about that I could handle, and it felt good. Yes, it was an escape. But it was more than an escape. After I went through the Mass or said my prayers I felt *good*. I really felt that if they killed me, at least I could go feeling good. I was ready to go. *Whatever happens today, at least I am ready to go*, I thought each morning, and each night I thought, *Well, I've made it through another day*.

If this sounds like a form of resignation, it is. In religious terms it might be called surrendering to the will of God. There lies the difference between a shrugging, swearing fatalism and the attitude needed to keep going. When you believe that there is the will of God behind everything, self-sacrifice has a meaning. I took this belief and the habit of prayer with me into interrogation and torture. If I couldn't almost literally rise above the brutal inducements to violate my code of conduct, if I had to yield to all too human weakness, I at least had the comfort that God was using me for some purpose.

Not long ago I was interviewed at my sons' Catholic school, Georgetown Prep in Rockville, Maryland. I attributed much of the strength that I needed to survive with honor to my Jesuit education—the basic philosophy, theology, ethics and self-discipline that it taught me. But I had to admit that it wasn't necessary to be a Christian, or a religious behavior of any kind, to adhere to the code of conduct we POWs set for ourselves. Those men without any professed religious convictions nonetheless subscribed to the concept that there was a higher good than self-preservation. One such was old-fashioned patriotism.

Perhaps naturally for men who had volunteered to serve their country in battle, all but a dozen of us thought that America was the greatest nation so far organized on earth. We thought that the war was a selfless, even if misguided, effort to share America's blessing of freedom with other peoples, and our experiences with the thinking and behavior of the rulers of North Vietnam confirmed this view. Going against the grain of self-preservation to resist them was more than a matter of national pride; it was a statement about the kind of people who come out of the American democratic system. We were aware of America's imperfections, spread before us daily by our captors in photographs and movies of social disruption. Typically, they would flash a picture of a peace march or demonstration in front of the White House and ask, "What do you think of that?" We always said, "That's not bad. That's good. It could only happen in a country like ours, a country where people have freedom to express themselves." Never had any of us valued freedom more than there in the dungeons of Hanoi.

A SPIRIT OF COOPERATION. Just as some of my fellow POWs stress better human relations as the benefit they derived from an otherwise bad experience, I stress human relations in the form of cooperation with others in the same enterprise when I talk to groups of employees or managers. At the Hanover Manufacturers meeting I boiled down my message to COMMU-NICATION, COOPERATION, GOAL SETTING. Once we worked out a means of communicating in our prison camps, we agreed on a command structure and established a goal of holding out until we could all return together in honor. I know that I personally could not have reached that goal without the co-operative support of the others, and I am sure that they would say the same. I wanted to kill myself when I finally broke down and signed enemy propaganda statements. What saved me were the confessions of others tougher and more senior than I that they had been forced to do the same. As Dick Stratton points out, we unwittingly took care of each other's guilt by communicating and cooperating.

One of the reasons that I take a stand on ethnic matters that isn't fashionable today is that dwelling on differences in race, skin color, national background gets in the way of cooperation. More than in any other area of American life, these distinctions are being phased out in the military, and they simply didn't exist in the Hanoi Hilton. The damage that they can do in weakening a group or a society was well appreci-ated by the North Vietnamese. They worked hard on me as a Mexican-American and Fred Cherry as a black to turn our supposed grievances as members of minorities into propa-ganda and betrayal of our prisonmates. If either of us had yielded we would have been left without honor and would have done incalculable damage to the others.

I don't urge young people like those Mexican-American students in Texas to band together to assert their rights. Instead I try to tell them that they will get their rights if they individually carry out their responsibilities, one of which is to get as much education as they can afford or absorb. I am proud of being living proof that America is a country in which a person can overcome economic disadvantages and ethnic stereotypes. Like my parents before me, and with even more justification than they had, I believe that education is the key to a successful and happy life in an open society. With that in mind, I oppose the movement to make Spanish (or any other foreign tongue) a second coequal language in American schools. This is a hindrance rather than a help to the young people who will eventually have to make their way in an English-speaking society. If you think about hyphenates like Mexican-American, Afro-American, Italian-American or whatever, you'll find that they tell the whole story from my point of view. The first word—Mexican in my case—represents the past; the second word—American in all cases—represents the present and future.

A FAITH IN ONE'S OWN INNER STRENGTH. I'm sometimes criticized for telling my audiences, after a recital of survival experiences, "You could do it, too!" The critics argue that the special circumstances of my life, or some innate form of will power, were responsible for my ability to take it. This won't wash. How then could you account for the fact that five hundred other men with their very different backgrounds and personalities managed to do the same? The critics also ignore a clause that I usually add to the statement: ". . . if you have a good set of basic values." Fortunately, most Americans are at least introduced to sound values at home, at school, in church. The message I bring is that, even if you haven't been consciously thinking about these values, they are there inside you to be called upon in time of crisis.

When I talked to psychologists and psychiatrists after my return, they seemed to marvel at the "techniques" I used to retain my sanity and deal with stress. They have even invited me to speak to their colleagues and students. It's flattering, but I had to confess to them that for the most part I didn't know what I was doing. Engineering, not psychology, has been my study and mental discipline. The techniques just came to me in the act of getting through each day. Like prayer, tears welled up and overflowed. I was brought up, as are most American boys, to believe that men don't cry. I'm here to tell you that's not true. In the first weeks and months I cried a lot—out of frustration at being helpless and hopeless. Shedding tears made me feel better. They seemed to have the effect of cleansing my mind so that I could concentrate on things I could do instead of on things I couldn't. When I developed means of positive thinking, the tears dried up. As I've reported earlier in this book, I finally lost the ability to cry. Now, however, I would advise letting go. I've indicated how grateful I was when the tears were able to come again.

The main cause of my early tears was thinking of what my capture and the lack of information about my fate must have been doing to my young wife and my family. My anxiety about them was almost intolerable until I started to suppress it, to "stuff it." I've learned later that psychologists differentiate between "suppression" and "repression." The former is normal and healthy; the latter can lead to illness. Suppression is a deliberate, conscious act. It's what's meant when we talk about putting something "on the back burner" in order to take care of what's cooking up front. Repression is a blacking out of an experience until it lives on only in the dark subconscious mind to haunt us. In effect, I said to myself, *It is pointless to agonize over my family since there is nothing I can do for or about them. I need all my emotional reserves to save myself.* It worked—almost too well, as the years it took me to unstuff myself attest.

Once I realized that the only thing I had control over was my own mind I started to make progress. The mind *is* a marvelous instrument, but we seldom hear its full range in the cacophony of modern life. We are too preoccupied with outside stimuli, with processing a load of current information, to listen to an inner voice. When all that is taken away, the mind comes into its own. I used it to invent rituals similar to prayer that would keep me usefully preoccupied.

Realizing that it was important to maintain the best health that I could, I began to allocate regular periods of time to physical conditioning by exercise. Hygiene was important, too. There wasn't much I could do about cleanliness in a rat- and vermin-infested cell with an open slop bucket. But what I could do, I did. I would use a piece of rag to clean one or two square tiles each day. Psychologically, it worked.

I also started reliving events in my life during a period that I set aside for this exercise in the later afternoon. I would reconstruct a day with all of its happenings minute-by-minute. During these sessions I tried to remember all the names of individuals associated with particular events, usually from school or college years. It was quite a challenge. I would summon up a group or class picture and then match names. I did pretty well, as I learned when I came home. I would bump into people I hadn't seen since childhood and surprise them by asking about brother "Jim" or sister "Mary" or whether their parents still lived on Sycamore Street. "How can you remember *that*?" they'd ask. Easy. Working at it saved my life.

Once I knew how valuable they could be, I developed other mental/physical exercises like playing chess with myself from scratch. I also spent long periods of time with an ear to a wall or an eye to a peephole, trying to make up for the deprivation of information. The extent to which I could broaden my frame of reference about the world outside my cell was remarkable. By adding an unseen or unheard "two" to the "two" caught by my senses of sound or sight I could often come up with "four." This helped in planning and bracing myself for what I might have to face in the way of, say, food or an interrogation. When we prisoners were finally in communication with each other, these observations became the stuff of the daily news.

Necessity also brought to the surface what I now regard as the handiest device for dealing with stress on all levels—a sense of proportion. When you don't know whether you are going to be living from one day to the next, it doesn't get any tougher than that. Mentally, if you made it through, you realize that life isn't that tough. Losing a job, having a child—sure, they're traumatic and tough—but you work your way through it. I guess I'll always use the jail cell as the standard. If we could work our way through that, we can work our way through this, whatever it is. My advice to people is that no matter how bad things are, they aren't as

bad as they could get. You have it in you to work it out. You
have got the ability in you and the strength of character in
you to get through these things day by day. If I did it, you can,
too. Stress is something that you can make as crippling as an
aching back if you let it get to you, but you can also make it
part of your challenge. I see dealing with stress as a day-to-
day challenge.

It's hard for any speaker or writer to know whether a message is getting across. In this I am fortunate in having a
constant touchstone. Fred Cherry and I have been returning
every year to Phil Straw's University of Maryland class where
it all began, and Phil keeps up to speed on audience reaction.
His own rather flip comment to a reporter on the effect of our
message—"I'll tell you, it's the last time I'll ever complain
about traffic on the beltway"—has important connotations
when applied to common, daily stress. More significant, perhaps, was his report in 1987 that inspired members of the
class organized themselves, raised money and built an impressive memorial to the Vietnam war veterans right next to
the chapel. But in the end, changing a single human mind is
the most gratifying reward of speaking out. Just as I was
beginning work on this book, I received a letter from a Maryland student named Paul Jung that I quote in part:

> You spoke to Mr. Straw's Honors class on October 9 of this
> year, and I would just like to convey how your comments
> affected me that evening. I am a philosophy major, and as an
> immigrant's son my secondary academic interest is in
> American values. As this fall semester began and as we sent
> more and more troops to the Middle East I talked with my
> father about what would happen if I got drafted. We came to
> the conclusion that I would go with pride. But then he
> added, 'Even if it was Vietnam, you would go.'
>
> Unfortunately, I had been thinking extensively about the
> failures of America. It was difficult not to, considering all
> the recent news—the S & L mess, Mayor Barry's drug trial,
> Irangate, the deficit, Japan, etc. America seemed to be going
> down the tubes, and with the events in Eastern Europe we

didn't seem like the one and only bastion of freedom in the world anymore. In fact, the reason why I'm taking Mr. Straw's class is because I want to examine one of our seemingly greatest mistakes, the Vietnam conflict. I loved America when I was growing up, but it didn't seem so great now. And to think that they would ask me to fight for it in a war? I had my doubts.

I talked it over with Mr. Straw after class the week before you came to talk with us. I couldn't resolve the conflict within myself, the fact that maybe I didn't believe in America anymore. He gave encouraging words, but I was still unresolved. Was I unpatriotic? None of my friends would have trouble avoiding the draft, especially my philosophy friends.

But then you and Colonel Cherry showed up. You both had me choked up because I just then realized that I had taken for granted what I failed to appreciate. America is still the best country, and I was only blinded by my spoiled and comfortable life. Maybe because you two were minority citizens like myself, or maybe just because you were genuinely proud, your words instilled in me the patriotism and pride that so badly needed boosting. I can say now, without regret or second thought, that I would gladly represent my country in any affair and in any capacity. I only hope that I can present as much honor with my life as you have with yours. I honestly thank you for waking me up."

Thank *you*,
Paul Jung.

CHAPTER XIV

On My Own

I HAD MORE BALLS in the air than a circus juggler in the last years of the 1980s. I was trying to get Marc on his feet— literally. Figuratively, I was trying to scramble onto my own feet financially by starting a business. I was writing a book. I was making speeches. Although I was officially out of government, I was up to my ears in politics. I was serving on several important advisory boards. If I hadn't been trying to practice what I was preaching in my writing and speaking, I would have dropped too many of these balls to make this story worth telling. But my theories about handling stress were being put to the acid test in my own life.

I tried to keep my personal problems in perspective in the harrowing fall of 1987. Things weren't really as bad as they could get, and thinking *should have, could have*—in Charlie Zuhoski's terms—wouldn't help. So I concentrated on the plans that Nick and Kevin and I were laying for a new business. Even when you are personally snagged in a backwater, life in general flows on. The Washington mainstream in those days was flowing in the direction of the 1988 elections that would determine the fate of the nation. Getting into that would not only take my mind off my own concerns but would also give me an opportunity to have some continuing influence on public policy. The same reasoning applied to my participation as a board member of various advisory groups in veterans' and military affairs.

One of the options open to me in the business world as a Mexican-American was to apply to the Small Business Administration (SBA) for accreditation under its Minority Small Business and Capital Ownership Development Program, known for short as the Section 8 (A) Program. This program is intended to give a "jump start" in securing government contracts to businesses with more than fifty percent of the ownership and the office of president and chief executive officer in the hands of a member of a designated minority—black, Hispanic or native American. It's designed to force a fledgling business to fly. If, for instance, fifteen percent of a company's business isn't outside the preferential work provided for by the program within four years, the company will no longer qualify under 8 (A). After nine years, the company is on its own.

At first I was reluctant to take advantage of this opportunity. It was certainly legal and legitimate, but would it be right for me? As a believer in helping people to help themselves, I couldn't quarrel with the premise of the program. Nor could I disagree with the historical evidence that the designated minorities had been disadvantaged in American society. Starting over at fifty, I needed any help I could get. None of us being wealthy, my partners and I would have to put our houses up at the bank to get the necessary capital. We agreed to turn all earnings back into developing the business until the books would justify drawing salaries for ourselves, if ever. This meant sentencing my family to an indefinite period of belt-tightening and more uncertainty. It would be unfair to everyone around me to indulge in foolish pride. I had used the GI bill to help finance my graduate education. Why not use this? If I thought that it might not be right to profit from an accident of birth, I also thought of the fact that I had lost eight and a half years of crucial career development as a POW and had surrendered retirement benefits for another six years to serve in government.

All this reasoning seemed sound, but I still might have held back except for one other factor—the 8 (A) program had a bad name. People who were misusing it threatened to kill off opportunity for people who really needed it. The long series of trials in the infamous Wedtech case was still going on. In the end, two congressmen and a legal adviser to Ed Meese, among many others, would be convicted and sentenced to jail on charges of bribery and extortion for "helping" an Hispanic minority firm in the Bronx in New York to get military contracts. Other 8 (A) businesses were known to be involved in unethical, if not illegal, practices. In view of all this, I told my prospective partners, "I'll apply for SBA accreditation on one condition—that our company be a model in every respect for how this program should work."

I knew that this wouldn't be easy, and so did my partners. Working for HCA, I had already discovered that the ethical climate out in the commercial world was very different from that in the military or government. The Navy's effort to turn us into officers and gentlemen didn't stop at showing me which fork to pick up. A system of values was both taught and demonstrated. Honesty, for example, was not the best policy; it was the *only* policy. Human nature being what it is, not everyone toed the line to the same degree. For me, the prison experience certified the worth of these values. I have trouble with my conscience if I speed a couple of miles over the limit at midnight on a back country road.

In government I found a similar ethic of honest service, but it was harder to adhere to. Everybody had his or her own agenda. In the way of politics, people were always maneuvering around each other, tripping each other, blocking each other. I saw questionable practices, and they bothered me. I'm the kind of person who likes to argue the merits of the case. If I win, fine; if I lose, OK. The point is to keep everything open and aboveboard. Since I couldn't change the kind of person I was, I decided that honesty was the only way I could avoid political pitfalls. This occasionally got me into hot water with the very people I was supposed to represent as a political appointee—the White House staff.

A continuing agenda of the Reagan administration was to cut the domestic budget. When I was acting administrator of the VA, the Office of Management and Budget got the bright idea of selling off excess government property, including some of the VA's. Normally, I'm for this kind of economy, but in this case I felt that the property was not "excess." Moreover, I felt fairly certain that the law prohibited sale of this particular property. I argued both points hotly with OMB, but I lost. The time came to defend the administration's budget on the Hill, and I went up to testify in its favor. When I was asked whether I thought it was a good idea to sell the VA property, I said, "No. Definitely not. It's a dumb idea. In ten years we'll be hurting for property in that area, and besides, the sale may be prohibited by law." Then came a good question: "Why did you put the item in the budget?" I could only reply, "I did my best to argue OMB out of it, but I lost." I was sure I could hear the OMB man sitting in on the hearings gasp. Needless to say, the property wasn't sold, but it may have been good for me that I was on my way out of the administration by then.

Out in the business world I found the predominant ethic to be that of competition—kill the other guy off, or if you can't beat him join him. As an athlete, I enjoy competition. I know it can be good for you; it keeps you sharp and motivated. But there's a fine line between healthy competition and unhealthy greed. On one side of that line you play openly by the rules; on the other, you tend to cheat. It can be hard to tell when you are crossing the line. For example, I learned that it was common practice in selling a program or a product to withhold information even from your bosses. It isn't actually lying, but it's not telling the whole truth. Is it honest? Probably not. I can't say that I haven't fallen into that trap, but I can say that I am very uncomfortable if I do. So I knew that the ethical goals my partners and I would be setting for ourselves in our new business would be as hard to reach as the financial ones.

From the beginning we would be accused of violating that competitive ethic of business. Since we would be 8 (A), other businesses would claim that we were getting a handout, a competitive edge. By competing fairly in all other respects we could do a lot to change the negative image of 8 (A) companies. Our pitch in selling ourselves would be: *We are going to operate with integrity. We are going to be open and honest. We are going to give you a good product. If we can't do that, we'll tell you. Or if we are going to have a problem doing it, we'll tell you. Our objective is to make you a happy customer, because a happy customer is a good customer, a steady customer.* With these principles agreed upon between us, Nick and Kevin and I found an existing company we could buy— Conwal, Incorporated—nursed it through the SBA accreditation process and opened its doors under new management on January 1, 1988.

Meanwhile my continuing interest in government was leading me ever deeper into political involvement. At the time I left the VA, I made a courtesy call on Vice-President Bush. The visit turned into a pleasant chat and photo op for both of us. "Look, I'd like to help you if you run for office in '88," I told him. "Thanks a lot," he said as we shook hands. While I was waiting to hear from Bush, Alexander Haig asked to see me in late '87. "Ev," he told me, "I'd really like you to join me in my run for President. There would be a big role for you in my campaign." I said I would think it over, and I did for a few days since I liked and respected Haig. But the prospect of taking on a "big role" while I was trying to get my business started was daunting, and I had made my promise to Bush. When I called to give Haig my decision, he was away, so I left a message with an aide: "Tell him I really appreciate being asked, but I have already promised George Bush." A few days later the aide returned my call. She was chuckling as she told me, "Mr. Haig said he understood, but then he asked, 'God, does he have to be so honest?' "

Besides keeping my word, I believed that Bush, with his experience as vice-president, would be the best man to manage the White House. Harry Walters and I had organized veterans for Reagan in '84, and by early spring '88 I was serving as an unpaid consultant in the same area for Bush headquarters. Luckily, the campaign was being run out of 755 15th Street, NW, just two blocks from the little office where I was still doing business as a consultant pending sufficient success with Conwal. I could drop in for a while every day to discuss strategy with the staffers. We all felt that getting out the veterans' vote would be more important this time around. Bush wasn't the shoo-in that Reagan had been, and strong veteran support would help to counter the so-called wimp factor. Eventually we organized a Veterans for George Bush Coalition with Sen. John McCain and I acting as cochairmen. Our function was to generate policies and support material for a network of veterans' organizations on the state level. In this, John and I acted as advisors to Ed Timberlake and his group, who were full-time staff members.

Our message and efforts were well-received by the veterans. For me, at least, it was a different story with the Hispanic Coalition that was right next to the Veterans Coalition in headquarters. The story would be instructive to anyone who thinks that there is a mystic ethnic-bonding within the American mix. For starters, Hispanic itself is a misnomer. Too often, people confusingly perceive it as a race. There are black and white Hispanics and all shades in between. There are Mexican, Puerto Rican, Cuban, Latin American Hispanics and some from Spain. There are Californian Hispanics, Texan Hispanics, Floridian Hispanics, Manhattan Hispanics. All of us are very human beings with all of the faults and hopefully some of the virtues of the heritage. One of these faults is shortsighted jealousy when it comes to protecting personal prerogatives and home turf, and it's there in ample supply in politics.

On my visits to Bush headquarters to deal with veterans' matters, I would go over and introduce myself to people working with Hispanics. I told them that I was well-known in California. Within the past year I'd had a high school named for me in Salinas and been inducted into the High School Hall of Fame at publicized ceremonies in San Diego. I offered to go out there and speak for the Bush/Quayle ticket. The offer was never accepted. One influential member of the group was a Mexican-American from Texas. He would sing out sarcastically when he saw me coming, "Ah! The big hero is here!" I ignored him. But, whatever his reasons, according to other members of the group he used his influence to stop them from sending me to California and, presumably, getting more publicity. Sad.

I was invited to take an even larger part in the 1988 Republican nominating convention in New Orleans than I had in 1984. In addition to leading the pledge of allegiance I led a prayer for those who had died in all wars while a bugler played taps. This time Tammy wasn't there with me since she was reluctant to leave the boys. Offstage, John McCain and I were busy entertaining veterans' groups and introducing them to people. In the wake of victory, a number of our campaign people got jobs in the administration, including Ed Timberlake, who became one of the assistant secretaries at the VA. There was also frequent mention of my name as a top candidate to be Secretary of Veterans Affairs, and that put me in a quandary.

A letter from George Bush gave substance to the talk. "Dear Everett," he wrote in October, "before the great memories of New Orleans get overtaken by the next big event I wanted to pause a moment to let you know how grateful I am for your contribution to the 1988 Convention program. The entire Bush family appreciates more than we can ever say the tremendous job you did for us. With friends like you by our side I know we will win in November!" Well, we did win, and friends are taken care of in politics. When the usually astute Washington *Post* speculated about my appointment, I had to come to grips with the fact that I would find it almost impossible to turn down a request from the President to lead a cause that was still very much a part of my life. But if the job were offered, there would undoubtedly be some very difficult decisions to be made about the business that Nick and Kevin and I were just getting under way.

I decided that I couldn't wait around in the dark. I knew Chase Untermeyer, who was Bush's choice as director of White House personnel. I tried to get through to him on the phone but never got a return call. I finally wrote a note asking point-blank whether I was a candidate for the position. In response I was sent a form for the data bank with such questions as: Are you a Republican? Did you work in the campaign? If so, at what level? Etc., etc. I knew then that I wouldn't have any agonizing choice to make. Perhaps rightly, they wanted all new people. The new Secretary of Veterans Affairs would be Edward J. Derwinski, a former colleague of Bush's in the House of Representatives, and I have continued to serve in a voluntary way as a member of the POW Advisory Board to the Secretary of Veterans Affairs, a board member of the Armed Services YMCA, a member of the Board of Regents of the Uniformed Services University of Health Sciences.

Perhaps I'm a glutton for punishment, but I expect to find some role to play in the next elections. I think that the political life of the country is too important to divorce myself from it. As I have so often said, I believe in the government of the United States. I have been critical of the antigovernment sentiment that developed in the sixties during the civil rights and Vietnam War controversies. My feeling is that the place to be critical of government is inside it, trying to make it work better. It has often been suggested that I get into politics as a candidate for elective office, most likely the House of Representatives. Having learned a good deal about life's surprises, I don't rule this out as a possibility. Holding public office is exciting and psychologically rewarding. But, as I have reason to know, doing a good job of it means a considerable sacrifice of private pleasures such as being with your family—and of privacy itself. Tammy and I have decided to hold off on any such commitment until the boys are away in college.

I am now grateful that the challenge and demands of a job like Secretary of Veterans Affairs passed me by at that critical time in my life, because it let me spend more time with my sons during their teen-age years. Even after he got to his feet at Thanksgiving time in 1987, Marc was still in pain and in need of a great deal of advice and encouragement to cope with his condition. He had to give up one of his favorite sports—skiing. He was good at golf but couldn't walk more

Family is still Number One on the Alvarez agenda. This picture was taken on the occasion of the publication of my first book, *Chained Eagle*. (The Washington *Post*)

than nine holes. Running and jumping on the hard floor in basketball hurt too much. Finally he settled on baseball. It didn't come naturally, and we spent many an evening at the batting cages giving him practice and instruction. I learned that this son was gifted with determination. Starting on the junior varsity, he spent the summer of sophomore year playing ball and made the varsity team in his junior year. He was also a straight-A student.

With Bryan I have a different but equally rewarding relationship. Also a very good student, he loves football and is good at it. I've been able to use my own experience as a player to help him. I don't want to imply that we have a perfect family. Especially at this writing, when Marc has discovered cars and girls, we have the kinds of father-son hassles that are the stuff of sitcoms. From me: "Get into the shower." "Don't argue with your mother." "Where were you?" From them: "Ah, gee, everybody else is going there/doing it, why can't we?" Although there are others, I cite this particular argument from the boys because developing a code of conduct begins with countering this kind of thinking. Win or lose, we keep after our sons to stick to the values they are exposed to at home, in church and in school. So far it seems we're winning.

FROM THE FIRST, running Conwal has presented daily moral challenges not unlike the business of raising children. There are plenty of temptations to give in and bend the rules, and the argument for doing so is usually the same as my boys'—everybody's doing it. I'm sure that giving in to that argument is what caused so many gifted and brilliant men on Wall Street to go astray. There were businesses who wanted us to "front" for them because we were minority-owned and could get contracts unavailable to them. There were individuals who offered to bring business to us for a fee. This can be done in legal ways, but there are also illegal ways, such as taking somebody on a contingency basis and giving him a certain percentage of a contract. There were people who proposed lying on the balance sheets and invoices. Whether the proposition was illegal or unethical, it was usually more lucrative than the aboveboard deal.

Our business contracts to supply the government with support services. Based on the collective talents of the three founders, we decided to focus on the areas of information management and specialized health programs, studies, and supports. We knew what we wanted to do, what we could do, but how could just three of us get started? Since we couldn't afford to hire people without a contract we lined up people with the skills we might need who would be willing to join us once we had work. Our first sale was to the Department of Labor. They wanted us to develop the architecture of the information system for the department's Grants Management Program. Labor was putting out many grants around the country through various offices, but it had no way of keeping track of them. With that contract in hand we were able to hire a director and staff, mostly computer-program people. And so it began. And so it still goes. Slowly, step by step.

Most of the unsavory but lucrative offers came to us in the first year or so. Perhaps the operatives just wanted to test the new kids on the block, or perhaps they could just smell how hungry we were. That year we grossed only $100,000, and none of us partners earned a cent. For health reasons Nick had to withdraw, and we were fortunate to find Marshall Nolan. He was not only willing to buy Nick's share but was in a position to bring us business. He had been running an operation much like ours—a five-person support unit for the Data Center of the Customs Service. I had no problem persuading my associates to pass up the deals that would keep us awake at night with guilty consciences, but Kevin recalls the perfectly legitimate Kodak proposition as the litmus test of our collective resolve.

In that period when we were still struggling, with no assurances whatever about our future, Kodak approached us to act as the distributor for a new product—a specialized hardened floppy disc. Except for a relationship to computers, the job had nothing to do with our business plan. But any association with as large and reputable a company as Kodak seemed worth exploring. As it unfolded in detail, the offer was stunning. They had the product, the marketing materials and several customers already lined up. By simply taking over distribution we would stand to earn between $500,000 and a million. But it would have meant raising another $250,000 or so on our personal assets to acquire a warehouse and cover marketing costs. In addition, handling a new product always involves high risk, and none of us had expertise in running distributorships. So, despite the lure of quick profit, I turned the offer down.

I'm still astonished by the results flowing from that and the rest of those early decisions to stick to our code and our plan. We grossed a million in 1989, and the partners were finally able to draw salaries and devote full time to Conwal. The figure was even better in 1990—$2,850,000. Our staff has grown from the original three to sixty. We have moved into the health-programs area, providing support for people who have been in the field a long time so they can do analyses in the areas of social disease and age-related programs. We also have a contract to run a data base for the Center for Disease Control. There is no artificial limit to growth in this business, and it's now a good bet that we will meet the 8 (A) schedule on time. There are times when my sleep is disturbed by pondering the problems presented by a job we've undertaken, but never by wondering whether we have been right in sticking to the high road.

WITH MY BUSINESS under control and my book *Chained Eagle* out and selling well, it began to look as if my life would settle into a pleasant suburban rut. This wasn't an unwelcome prospect after all my family and I had been through. Then along came war in the Persian Gulf. Like millions of other Americans, I couldn't tear myself away from the television set. I remember watching the first strikes on Baghdad with the tracers coming up and feeling that I was right in the cockpit. In the middle of it the phone rang. It was my sister Delia. "God, this is *déjà vu*. We're living the whole thing over again," she said. She couldn't begin to know how true her words were for me. And when the battered face of the first POW appeared on screen, seventeen years fell away, and I felt the old fear. The phone was ringing again—and again. It was the media wanting comment. I was again in the public eye.

For a week or more I suspended doing business as usual and devoted most of my time to television and radio interviews locally and nationally. I was glad to have the opportunity to speak out, to try to get across many of the things I've said in this book. My main objective in these interviews was to reassure families about the POWs in Iraq. The very fact that their pictures had been shown on TV was almost a guarantee of their survival. Iraq was admitting to the world that they were in custody and would have to account for them later. As for the statements they were giving, here's the gist of what I told my interviewers:

"When a person is lucky enough to get shot down without injuries, it's bad enough. But can you imagine what it's like with injuries? He's got that to deal with. I'm sure they aren't getting the best of medical care. These people are particularly vulnerable in a state of shock, operating at a high level of adrenalin. That will continue for days or weeks. Obviously, they are in confusion. Then they're getting beaten by their captors. At first they will try to get military information. But it's interesting how quickly they work to get propaganda statements. You can see by their faces and the way they are that they are resisting. You can bet your life they're being tortured. Obviously, the Iraqis wanted these statements fast. There are means that the enemy can use to get anything out of you. People are surprised how fast they are coming out with statements. I'm not—we're not, the guys who were POWs. Keep behind those guys and let them know that we love them, we support them, and we want them back."

I don't know how much my message helped, but the American people did stay behind the whole force in the Gulf, POWs included. When the Navy and Marine POWs were repatriated to Bethesda Naval Hospital outside Washington, I was asked to meet with them. It was a curious event. They were so young that I was a figure out of long-past history, if they'd heard of me at all. Learning how long I had been in captivity, they were more interested in hearing my story than in telling their own. They seemed in good shape and spirits. But out of my experience I had one important piece of advice for them: speak freely to your family and friends, share your own feelings and encourage them to share theirs. Healing begins with understanding. As I well knew, easier said than done.

People have often asked me for my opinion on the MIA situation. I am no expert on this matter. I can say that our communication system throughout the prisoner of war complex in North Vietnam was so good that we were able to account for every American who was brought into Hanoi's orbit. As for those held elsewhere, it may be a different story. Having experienced the sometimes strange quirks of the Vietnamese mind, I wouldn't rule out any possibility. I doubt there are any living Americans being held against their will. Nevertheless, I can appreciate more than most the hope that won't die in the families of Americans still unaccounted for. So I believe that every effort should be made to run down rumors of sightings and to investigate fully such phenomena as the picture of three alleged POWs that was being published at the time of this writing. If these are hoaxes, they are the cruelest I can imagine, and they must be laid to rest, one way or another.

MY OWN HEALING has not been complete. From the very first, I kept telling the press and audiences that I was not bitter about my experience, that I had no hatred for my enemies. At least on the conscious level I believe I was sincere in saying this. To be sure, there were brutal individuals among the guards, men who reveled in their work of torture, and I would admit to hating them. But such individuals can be found in any society and at any time. For the most part our guards were misfits in their society, men who for one reason or another couldn't qualify for service at the front or in higher posts of government. They and most of the people we glimpsed in the streets and fields really were to be pitied more than hated. Along with us, they were victims of a torturing, cruel system. While I could honestly say that I wasn't conscious of any hatred in my heart, I almost always added the emphatic statement that I had no desire ever to see Vietnam again—or to meet any Vietnamese.

I guess I was still "stuffing it." If I stayed away wouldn't that chapter in my life just close itself? It was much easier to handle it as something that had happened in the past, a story of good guys versus bad guys with a beginning and an end rather than think of it as part of an ongoing human drama in which the actors could change their masks. I admired John

McCain, who had the toughness of mind to return to Hanoi to investigate the Missing in Action problem as part of his senatorial duty. But I wasn't interested. I had enough to do, didn't I? With a life like mine, I should know better.

Toward the end of the writing of this book I was invited to lunch by Fred Downes, director of the VA's prosthetics department. A Vietnam vet and an amputee, Fred had been to North Vietnam many times as part of the group working with the MIA situation. He invoked a lot of memories by telling me how he had walked around the outside of the Hanoi Hilton. He started me thinking when he talked about how his own hatred for the enemy was dissolving in contact with what he now saw as a gentle people. I couldn't resist a few nights later when Fred asked me to go with him to a reception in a Washington home for Lê Bang, Deputy Director for the Department of American Affairs in the Vietnamese Foreign Ministry.

A small man of about my age, Lê Bang seemed as interested in me as I was in him. We hadn't met in my time in Hanoi, but he knew of me. Artifacts from my plane are still on exhibition in a war museum in Hanoi. He accepted a signed copy of *Chained Eagle* and we sat down to talk. I can't say we had a meeting of minds, but we at least were able to carry on a civil exchange. He expressed great admiration for the American people, but he clearly separated the people from the government. I told him that in America the government *is* the people. I said that there would be no real rapprochement between our governments or peoples until his government was more forthcoming on the MIA question.

As I was leaving, Lê Bang invited me to come to Hanoi. For the first time I didn't have a knee-jerk reaction. I didn't say "No!" This man seemed reasonable. I retain a skepticism about what might be behind the placid Vietnamese facade. But if Lê Bang is really representative of Vietnamese attitudes today, I might well find myself dealing with the future rather than the past on a visit to Hanoi. What I told Lê Bang was that I would return to Vietnam when and if I could make it part of some constructive cause. This is beginning to develop. Senator McCain's wife, for instance, was in the process of organizing a medical group to go to Vietnam even as Lê Bang and I were talking. I have no doubt that the right call will come along for me. I have no doubt that the day of final healing of the wounds of Vietnam for me, and for this nation, is at hand.

EPILOGUE

A Credo

MY PERSONAL CODE, the belief that sustained me through eight and a half years as a prisoner of war in North Vietnam, is built on the solid rock of the Scout Oath that I took as a boy in Salinas, California.

ON MY HONOR ...

I prize nothing higher than honor, which for me is my word, my integrity, my reputation. To be honorable is to be honest—say what you mean—and to be trustworthy—do what you say. An honorable person is by definition a reliable person. The goal we POWs set for ourselves in captivity was to return home with honor intact, and the means we used to reach that goal was relying on each other's honor. After an experience like that, you know how powerful swearing by your honor can be.

I WILL DO MY BEST ...

When the going got rough, I learned to tell myself: *Don't quit. Give it your best shot. Make an honest attempt.* Nobody can endure everything, achieve everything. At some point in time and under some form of duress each one of the 500 of us POWs reached his breaking point. In order to make it effective and realistic, we had to shorten the military code of conduct to the essence of the Scout Oath—do your best. It then became possible to keep the code, and in most cases our best was better than any of us thought it could be. I believe you only do your best when you set your goals higher than you feel you can reach.

TO DO MY DUTY . . .

Duty isn't what I'm told to do but what I know I have to do— my responsibility, my obligation, what I owe. My grandmother, who learned everything she had the hard way, passed her work ethic down to me. I still bless her for it. The price of freedom and independence is a sense of responsibility. The payoff for accepting responsibility is healthy pride. I worked hard to get where I am, and I feel that I earned my place in life. It's a good feeling but one that must be re-earned every day.

TO GOD . . .

Yes, I work hard, but it is God who provides. I believe in Him. He preserved my life when it should have been lost. He took care of me when I was powerless to do for myself. He has watched over my loved ones when they have been beyond my reach and help. I need God. I am human, with the weaknesses and faults that go with being human. Since God has not given up on me, I must not give up on Him. So I try to do my duty through worship and obedience to His commands as I understand them.

AND MY COUNTRY . . .

I see country as more than a form of political organization or a geographical area or a conglomerate of people. I see country as community—neighbors, comrades in arms, friends, family. I exist as a part of that community; apart from it, I am reduced. In the service, in captivity, I found that I was willing to die for my country, and I still am. But the kind of country I believe in emerges from sharing values. I grew up in the

There is, perhaps, no more concrete evidence of the value of a life lived by a code of conduct than this sign my family posed behind on a trip to California. When it was put up shortly after my return from North Vietnam, the mayor of Santa Clara told me, "Don't mess up, Ev. If you do we'll have to change the sign." It is still there.

Scouts, in the church, in school, in the Navy believing that being an American meant roughly the same thing to all of us *no matter where our ancestors came from.* That's why it was so wounding to me to experience the divisiveness of America when I came home from Vietnam, why I am now concerned about the movement toward ethnic enclaves. I believe my duty to the country that gave me such great opportunities is to see that it becomes more—not less—of a community.

Saying you have a code, a system of belief, is not, of course, the same as practicing it. Over the years I have developed a simple test to determine whether I am living by my code. If I can look myself in the eye in the mirror and sleep through the night without twinges of conscience, I know that I have managed to get through one more day with honor. That's the best, and least, I can do.

INDEX

229